BY TH
MEET VERA
STARK

BY LYNN NOTTAGE

★

★

DRAMATISTS
PLAY SERVICE
INC.

BY THE WAY, MEET VERA STARK
Copyright © 2013, Lynn Nottage

All Rights Reserved

SPECIAL NOTE

SPECIAL NOTE ON SONGS AND RECORDINGS

BY THE WAY, MEET VERA STARK was originally produced by Second Stage Theatre (Carole Rothman, Artistic Director; Casey Reitz, Executive Director) in New York City, opening on May 9, 2011. It was directed by Jo Bonney; the set design was by Neil Patel; the costume design was by ESosa; the lighting design was by Jeff Croiter; the sound design was by John Gromada; the film of *The Belle of New Orleans* was by Tony Gerber; the dialect coach was Stephen Gabis; the projections were by Shawn Sagady; the production stage manager was Lori Ann Zepp; the associate artistic director was Christopher Burney; the production manager was Jeff Wild; and the general manager was Don-Scott Cooper. The cast was as follows:

VERA STARK . . . . Sanaa Lathan
GLORIA MITCHELL . . . . Stephanie J. Block
LOTTIE/CARMEN . . . . Kimberly Hébert Gregory
ANNA MAE/AFUA ASSATA EJOBO . . . . Karen Olivo
LEROY BARKSDALE/HERB FORRESTER . . . . Daniel Breaker
FREDRICK SLASVICK/BRAD DONOVAN . . . . David Garrison
MAXMILLIAN VON OSTER/
PETER RHYS-DAVIES . . . . Kevin Isola

BY THE WAY, MEET VERA STARK received its West Coast premiere at the Geffen Playhouse on September 18, 2012. It was directed by Jo Bonney; the set design was by Neil Patel; the costume design was by Esosa; the lighting design was by Jeff Croiter; the sound design was by John Gromada; and the film of *The Belle of New Orleans* was by Tony Gerber. The cast was as follows:

VERA STARK	Sanaa Lathan
GLORIA MITCHELL	Amanda Detmer
LOTTIE/CARMEN	Kimberly Hébert Gregory
ANNA MAE/AFUA ASSATA EJOBO	Merle Dandridge
LEROY BARKSDALE/HERB FORRESTER	Kevin T. Carroll
FREDRICK SLASVICK/BRAD DONOVAN	Spencer Garrett
MAXMILLIAN VON OSTER/ PETER RHYS-DAVIES	Mather Zickel

CHARACTERS

VERA STARK

GLORIA MITCHELL

LEROY BARKSDALE/HERB FORRESTER *

LOTTIE McBRIDE/CARMEN LEVY-GREEN *

ANNA MAE SIMPKINS/AFUA ASSATA EJOBO *

MR. SLASVICK/BRAD DONOVAN *

MAXMILLIAN VON OSTER/PETER RHYS-DAVIES *

* Characters should always be double cast.

SETTING

Hollywood, 1933, 1973, 2003.

NOTE

In the tradition of the screwball comedies of the 1930s, Act One should be very fast-paced, whimsical and always buoyant. Breathless. Act Two should be no less fast-paced, but should reflect the comic sensibilities of 1973 and 2003.

// indicates places where dialogue overlaps.

For the final act of the play please visit www.meetverastark.com and www.findingverastark.com

BY THE WAY, MEET VERA STARK

ACT ONE

Scene 1

A living room. Deco stylish. Hollywood, 1933.

Gloria Mitchell, 28, "white" starlet, in a dressing gown, lies across the couch nursing a healthy glass of gin.

Vera Stark, 28, an African-American beauty wearing a maid's uniform, tentatively enters. She pauses, then ventures to speak.

VERA. *(With Southern accent.)* Mis', Mr. Lafayette here to see ya. *(Gloria registers shock and dismay.)*
GLORIA. *(With sweet girlish Southern accent.)* Tell him I'm not here. I can't bear to face him, not like this, not now, not after all that has happened.
VERA. But, he already know ya here. Dat rascal Cassius dun tol' him.
GLORIA. Tell him to go. Tell him I'm sleeping. Tell him anything. I can't. No. No. I don't want to see him.
VERA. He ain't want me to say, but he missing ya sum'ting awful —
GLORIA. Oh, won't you tell him to go already! *(Vera reluctantly turns to leave.)* Wait. *(Tenderly.)* Does he look well?
VERA. He look real good, Mis'. *(Gloria smiles, wrestling with what to say.)*

GLORIA. Did he bring azaleas?

VERA. You know he always do. *(Gloria gasps dramatically.)*

GLORIA. And does he know? Did you tell him I'm dying? *(Gloria coughs.)*

VERA. I don't know, what he know. But I do know dat he here. Miss, dat man out dere love you. And if you send him away now, it gonna be a real shame. Ya can't keep hiding from de worl'. Talk to him, tell him how ya feel. Tell him ya love him. 'Cause ya and I know dere ain't no other man in your heart but him.

GLORIA. How do you put up with me? *(Gloria reaches out for Vera's hand.)*

VERA. Mis', whatcha want me to tell him? *(A long pause, Gloria is thinking.)* Whatcha want me to tell him? *(Another long pause. Irritated.)* Whatcha want me to tell him?

GLORIA. *(Dropping the southern accent.)* Oh damn. What the hell am I supposed to tell him? *(Vera stares at Gloria, then consults the film script tucked away in her apron.)* Oh, give me the line already …

VERA. Tell him —

GLORIA. Wait! *(Gloria presses her fingers to her forehead, finally — With accent. Excited.)* Tell him to remember me on that warm summer —

VERA. *(Correcting.)* Spring —

GLORIA. — Day we went boating on the bayou. I was wearing that blue —

VERA. *(Correcting.)* Violet.

GLORIA. Sweater —

VERA. *(Correcting.)* Cardigan.

GLORIA. *(Exasperated — dropping accent.)* Oh God, how am I supposed to remember these lines? They just pour out of my head like water. I reach for them and they're gone. It's impossible. I can't do it. *(Gloria stands theatrically.)* These words. "Sweater." "Cardigan." Who gives a goddamn? The woman is dying, why does she have to make so many speeches about it?

VERA. Because that's what's written, honey. And as you know, the writer likes for you to say what's written. That's how it works.

GLORIA. Oh, I know that. Don't you think I know that? *(Vera snatches the glass out of Gloria's hand, and sniffs it.)*

VERA. Gin? Now, let's do it again. *(Gloria snatches the glass back.)*

GLORIA. The indignity, really! Why should I have to screen test for this film? I've played this role, I practically invented it. Tragic

Jane with consumption, Lydia with the hole in her fragile heart, and who can forget poor stupid little Maybelle who was slowly being poisoned by her diabolical, but "winsome" husband.

VERA. Yes, we know! But honey, this is different. It's Marie, *(Grandly.)* "the Belle of New Orleans." I don't have to tell you, every actress with halfway good teeth wants this role. And believe me, they'll do whatever it takes to get it. *(Vera suggestively wipes the corners of her mouth, and slaps her butt.)*

GLORIA. Hussies, I bet they will. Shame on them.

VERA. Now c'mon, pull yourself together, won't ya. And remember what Maestro used to say in New York.

GLORIA. Yeah, yeah, the king of the pratfall dispensing wisdom like pellets of cyanide.

VERA. Then, never mind. I have a half-dozen things I can be doing. *(Vera ventures to leave.)*

GLORIA. Where are you going? Vera! Vera! Vera! *(Gloria grabs the script.)* Okay, okay. Wait. Yes, I love him, but all I can think about is "boating on the bayou," and how utterly ridiculous that sounds. *(Gloria tosses the script.)*

VERA. Then, missie, think about the fact that you'll be working with the most important director in pictures.

GLORIA. Important? Von Omelette or whatever his name is, the man barely speaks English. Important? Says who?

VERA. Says the people who pay for all of this. The studio. Your agent. Everyone! But who are they?

GLORIA. Oh blah, blah, blah. I don't want to hear anymore.

VERA. I'm not gonna argue with you, honey. Tick-tock, it's already one o'clock.

GLORIA. *(Panicked.)* What? No, no. It … It can't be.

VERA. Tick-tock. One-oh-one.

GLORIA. No. No, it can't be. Won't you call Alfred and have him put this off until tomorrow. I'm not ready. Tell him I have a fever, I'm —

VERA. Ready or not, you're due at the studio in an hour, and we haven't even gotten you dressed yet. Remember what Alfred said, there won't be a next time if you don't show up on time.

GLORIA. *(Overly dramatic.)* You're being overly dramatic. You're making me nervous. I'm feeling faint. *(Gloria makes a dramatic show of growing faint. Vera is unmoved.)*

VERA. If you're late, don't blame it on me. And I shouldn't really say —

GLORIA. *(Suddenly alert.)* What?

VERA. Oh nothing, there's just been some talk.

GLORIA. Talk? Who? // What are they saying? *(Vera actively ignores Gloria, who does her best to pretend she doesn't care.)*

VERA. I promised myself I wouldn't —

GLORIA. Oh, don't be coy. Spill it! *(Vera holds out the dish of chocolates. Gloria digs into the dish and bites into a chocolate.)* Mmmm.

VERA. Well, it seems people at the studio have been gossiping, and ... and —

GLORIA. And?

VERA. And —

GLORIA. And? Yes? *(Gloria grabs another chocolate from the dish, and pops the chocolate into her mouth.)*

VERA. They're questioning when, if ever, you'll lose the baby fat. *(Gloria sucks in her gut and spits out the chocolate.)*

GLORIA. Ha! The nerve of them. I'll have you know some women wear baby fat well into their thirties.

VERA. But it appears you're wearing it rather more comfortably than they'd like. Umm-hmm.

GLORIA. How dare them! *(Gloria lights a cigarette and regains her composure. Vera drapes a glamorous green gown over the couch.)* Baby fat?! I'm not the least bit bothered. Well, I don't care! I'm "America's Little Sweetie Pie." *Photoplay* called me one of the most beautiful "young" starlets on the scene.

VERA. Yeah, swell article, honey. I remember reading it five years ago.

GLORIA. Don't talk to me! Don't you dare talk to me! Honestly. And I've told you I'm not wearing the green dress. I wore that to an opening three weeks ago, and everyone made such an awful fuss. It will seem redundant. Oh, bring me the red dress already.

VERA. The red makes you look coquettish.

GLORIA. Coquettish? Where ever did you learn that word? *(Vera smiles with a sense of satisfaction.)*

VERA. Did you read the script?

GLORIA. Of course I did! ... Well, I read my lines.

VERA. If you'd bothered to read the entire script, you'd know that Marie's not supposed to appear "coquettish."

GLORIA. Who cares? I think the red says warmth and fire.

VERA. Or that you're horny and desperate.

GLORIA. So?

VERA. You're playing a dying virgin.

GLORIA. *(Beneath her breath.)* All the more reason to be horny and desperate, don't you think?

VERA. Then do what you'd like. I'll go "fetch" the red dress. *(Vera makes a show of leaving.)*

GLORIA. Whatever is the matter with you?

VERA. How much time do you got?

GLORIA. Oh, what are you prattling on about?

VERA. Um … did you —

GLORIA. Yes?

VERA. Mention —

GLORIA. What?

VERA. Well, the role of Tilly, you said they're casting Tilly the maid, and, and, and, you know, well, I know the role and —

GLORIA. And, and, and, you know. What are you asking?

VERA. You promised you'd put in a word with the studio.

GLORIA. Oh Vera, I have so many things to worry about. Why on earth are you bothering me with this?

VERA. Never mind. I'll go "fetch" the dress.

GLORIA. Oh boo-hoo. Sometimes it would do you a bit of good to remember the distance you've travelled from there to here.

VERA. You'll never let me forget, honey. Will you? And you might remember there's a lot I could say about your daddy, my mother's —

GLORIA. Then say it already and let's be done with it.

VERA. Is that what you really want? *(Gloria rolls her eyes and pretends to be unfazed.)*

GLORIA. Enough, Vera. I'm tense as it is. And really, no one has ever been a hundred percent sure he was my daddy.

VERA. And what exactly does that say about your mother? *(Gloria feigns shock. Gasps.)*

GLORIA. Vera Stark, you're wearing far too much wicked this morning.

VERA. Oh, hush your mouth, and go put on this dress. *(Gloria feigns exhaustion.)*

GLORIA. *(Truthfully.)* I'm feeling rather fragile, would you mind being a little kinder to me? Darling. Friends?

VERA. I'm all hugs and kisses. I adore you, really. *(Vera gives Gloria a perfunctory hug.)* There! Now, honey, whatcha want me to tell him?

GLORIA. *(Affecting an emotional Southern accent.)* Tell him to remember me on that warm spring day we went boating on the bayou. I was wearing that violet cardigan that Mammy made. It was a perfect afternoon, as perfect as it could be. And if he remembers, as I do, we didn't ever want it to end. I like to think of us that way. *(Gloria smiles.)* HA!

VERA. Go! *(Gloria grabs the green dress and exits with a flourish. Vera smiles triumphantly.)*

Scene 2

Radio. A flourish of dramatic suspenseful music.

A slightly dishevelled bachelorette apartment.

Lottie, 20s, a pretty, heavy-set brown-skinned woman, meticulously sews labels into men's shirts, as she listens to a radio program.

RADIO ACTOR. *Mary Cavendish, don't walk away from me, I know exactly what you're thinking.*

LOTTIE. Umm-hmm.

RADIO ACTOR. *Say what you will, but, darling, I smelled the wicked scent of deception the moment you walked in here. Does the name Laurel Price mean anything to you? No, no, don't answer, I will find out the truth soon enough.*

LOTTIE. Careful, Arthur, she's playing you.

RADIO ACTOR. *Mary? … Mary! What are you doing?*

LOTTIE. Uh-oh. Don't trust her.

RADIO ACTOR. *Why are you pointing that wretched thing at me? Mary … NO! (A gunshot. Lottie gasps loudly. A dramatic flourish of music.)*

RADIO ANNOUNCER. *And that brings down the curtain on this evening's program, brought to you by the gentle cool refreshing taste of Gold Country cigarettes. The number one healthy choice for America's most discerning smokers. (A commercial jingle. Vera enters in a flurry, winded.)*

VERA. It over? What did I miss?

LOTTIE. It just ended.

VERA. Oh, heck. Was it good?

LOTTIE. Honey, he finally found out what she was up to and —

VERA. Don't tell me. Damn it, why does something good always happen when I'm late? *(The radio, softly jazzy, plays the hits of the day.)*

LOTTIE. Where you been?

VERA. Oh, where do you think? At the studio making sure Gloria didn't piss on herself. *(Vera takes off her shoes, and tosses them across the room.)*

LOTTIE. Did you remember to bring me ciggies? *(Vera reluctantly picks up her shoes, then takes six cigarettes from her blouse.)* How much I owe ya?

VERA. Nothing, I pinched them from Gloria.

LOTTIE. Thanks, honey. *(Lottie lights a cigarette. As she speaks, Vera loosens her blouse and unwinds.)*

VERA. Hey Lottie, you're never gonna believe what happened. The streetcar got stopped on Central, there was nearly a riot. The police were swarming all over the place. Heard someone say a fella got stabbed at the market. They were plucking Negroes off the streetcar like cotton.

LOTTIE. There's always something going on down there. Did they catch 'em?

VERA. I didn't bother to stick around to ask. Got a ride with Dottie's man. You know, the gimpy porter from Sacramento. *(Music continues on the radio.)* What's playing? I just love this song. Turn it up. *(Vera sways to the music.)*

LOTTIE. Only if you want to trade blows with the loudmouth across the hall.

VERA. She home?

LOTTIE. Yup.

VERA. Don't she have any place to go?

LOTTIE. I guess someone that evil don't get invited out much. *(Vera impatiently watches Lottie sew.)* What? Go on, ask.

VERA. … Did the casting agency call?

LOTTIE. Nope.

VERA. You sure?

LOTTIE. Let me think … Yup, I'm sure. Sorry, honey. *(Anna Mae, a very, very, fair-skinned African-American woman, enters dressed to kill. She frantically rushes through the room readying herself for the evening.)*

VERA. Where is she — ? *(Anna Mae exits as quickly as she entered.)*

LOTTIE. Ignore her, she's been driving me crazy all afternoon. *(Anna Mae reenters like a whirlwind.)*

VERA. Hey.

ANNA MAE. Oh, hey Vera.

VERA. Where are you going all spiffed up? *(Anna Mae, demonstratively, twirls.)*

ANNA MAE. The double D, darling. Dinner and dancing.

LOTTIE. She's got a date.

VERA. Tonight? Who? He must be something, looks like you broke out the expensive rags. Let me see. *(Anna Mae shows off her dress, doing a sexy shimmy.)*

ANNA MAE. I beg your pardon, he's a little more than something. Thank you. He's a genuine movie director.

LOTTIE. Like that last one.

ANNA MAE. Oh, go to hell. He's the real deal this time. I met him at the studio on Tuesday.

LOTTIE. Oh, you just happened upon him?

ANNA MAE. Shut your mouth. *(To Vera.)* I was on a ciggie break. He gave me a light. Don't hate me girls, but he called me Thursday, again on Friday and then again on Saturday, but I didn't get the message until this morning 'cause that hussy across the hall's been sitting on my messages. Anyway, I only said yes 'cause he showed up outside in his Dusenberg, and I ain't gonna lie to ya, I ain't never seen the inside of a Dusenberg. *(Anna Mae strikes a sexy pose.)* Whatcha think? Huh?

LOTTIE. It's a little snug.

ANNA MAE. Good. Help me, will ya? *(Vera buttons her up, then tucks the label into the back of her dress.)* Hey Lottie, let me borrow your fox stole.

LOTTIE. Hell no, you ain't wearing my stole.

ANNA MAE. Oh, c'mon, don't be so damn stingy. I'll loan you my lavender heels.

LOTTIE. Them ancient shoes. Nah, ma'am.

ANNA MAE. Last I'll ask.

LOTTIE. No, no, no and no again. I worked too damn hard for my fox tail. That stole my pinched pennies, and I ain't forget how ya made fun of it.

ANNA MAE. I was kidding ya. *(To Vera.)* Tell her I was kidding.

LOTTIE. Ha, ha, ha, no!

ANNA MAE. C'mon. And really, when was the last time you wore the darn thing.

LOTTIE. I may never wear it, but that don't mean you will.

ANNA MAE. Vera.

VERA. This is between you two.

LOTTIE. I said no!

ANNA MAE. *(All sweet.)* Vera, honey, can I borrow your coat?

VERA. Why don't you buy yourself a dress coat already?

ANNA MAE. With what money?

VERA. The same money I ain't got.

ANNA MAE. Please. How am I gonna go out here without a proper evening coat?

LOTTIE. Well, that surely ain't my problem. You should have thought about that while you were spending your money on cigarettes and fan magazines, sugar.

ANNA MAE. After all I done for you?

LOTTIE. All you done for me? Vera, talk to this girl.

ANNA MAE. Please, Vera. I'll owe you. Last I'll ask.

VERA. Oh, all right, it's in the closet. And don't sweat it up.

ANNA MAE. Thank you, honey.

VERA. I just got it back from the cleaners.

ANNA MAE. I'll take precious good care of it. I will. You're an angel. *(She sticks her tongue out at Lottie, and turns to leave.)*

VERA. Hey, Anna Mae, before I forget, Gloria is having a dinner party next Saturday and Beulah's daughter is getting married so she can't help out. Are you interested in picking up a little something extra for your pocket?

ANNA MAE. Oh … I'd love to, honey, but I promised Grace I'd take her shift. *(Anna exits in a flurry.)*

LOTTIE. How come you didn't ask me?

VERA. Because I know how you feel about Gloria.

LOTTIE. That don't mean I won't take her money.

ANNA MAE. *(Offstage.)* Has anyone seen my jar of cold cream?

VERA. No.

LOTTIE. Here it comes.

ANNA MAE. *(Offstage.)* Vera, may I use yours? You won't even notice I took any.

VERA. Sure, honey. *(To Lottie.)* This hussy's been out every night this week. *(Vera does the shimmy dance.)*

LOTTIE. You ain't kidding. She's courting trouble and a permanent hangover. Don't tell her I told you, but they gave her another talking-to at work.

VERA. What she done?

LOTTIE. Whatcha think? She's been shaking her sassy behind around the director's lounge. Chatting up the swells.

VERA. Again?

LOTTIE. Gal genuinely believes one of those white men is gonna put her in a picture. *(Vera laughs. The buzzer rings.)*

VERA. *(Shouts.)* You want me to run down and get it?

ANNA MAE. *(Offstage.)* No! No! I'll get it. *(Vera moves for the door. Anne Mae comes racing in, nearly knocking Vera over on the way to the door.)* I said, I'll get it!

VERA. All right. All right. What's with her?

LOTTIE. He don't know she colored.

VERA. Ya lyin'.

LOTTIE. Am I? Ask her.

VERA. OOO-WEE. This has the makings of a might good tragedy. *(Anna Mae puts on Vera's coat.)*

ANNA MAE. Only in the movies, sugar, only in the movies. In real life, one Anna Mae Simpkins gets to eat clams on a half shell, sip champagne from crystal and dance all night to the Starlight Orchestra. *(Anna Mae winks.)*

LOTTIE. Ask her where she's from?

ANNA MAE. *(With accent.)* Rio De Janiero.

VERA. And when he finds out the truth?

ANNA MAE. He'll have his fingers too deep into this honey pot to let it go. Just out for a little fun. Don't wait up, girls. I'll fill you in tomorrow morning. *Adeus bebe. (Anna Mae blows a kiss and leaves.)*

LOTTIE. One of these days it's gonna rain real trouble on that gal. There are half a dozen upright Negroes chasing her straight ass hair, and she's dipping into dives with any ofay that'll toss her a nickel. *(Lottie rushes to the window.)*

VERA. How does he look?

LOTTIE. Horny as hell and up to no damn good.

VERA. He old?

LOTTIE. Nah, and look at that, he's definitely more refined than her usual pocketbook. I ain't gonna say he's good-looking, but he ain't hard on the eye.

VERA. What's he doing?

LOTTIE. He's holding the door for her. Oh God, she's doing that thing she does with her hair. Oh, stop it already, and get into the car, will ya. *(Shouts.)* Get in, hussy! *(Lottie laughs. Vera tries to sneak a script out of her bag.)* Ooo. There they go. *(Lottie catches Vera mid-action.)* What's that you got there?

VERA. Oh, nothing. *(Vera tries to hide the script behind her back.)*

LOTTIE. Nothing? You got something there. What? What is it?

VERA. Um. Just a script.

LOTTIE. *(Hyper-interest.)* A script? What for?

VERA. Oh, um ... a Southern epic. Nothing. You know, Gloria's testing for the lead. It's nothing.

LOTTIE. A Southern epic?

VERA. Yup.

LOTTIE. And just why are you so interested in it?

VERA. A Southern epic! Magnolias and petticoats. You know what else it means, cotton and slaves —

LOTTIE. *(Perks up.)* Slaves? With lines?

VERA. Slaves with lines, honey.

LOTTIE. Yeah? So is there a part in it for me? *(Sings.)*
    Go down Moses
    Way down in Egypt's land
    Tell ol' Pharaoh,
    Let my people go.

VERA. You can put away the big voice, it's not a musical.

LOTTIE. A dramatique?! I betcha that's what those gals was whispering about at the market. Sneaky little wenches. I knew they was up to something. A Southern epic! So, talk to me, honey.

VERA. Well, it's the story of a beautiful octoroon, who falls hopelessly in love with a white merchant. She contracts scarlet fever —

LOTTIE. Of course!

VERA. And she's dying, but ... but must alas pretend not to love the merchant in a selfless attempt to shield him from the truth about her race.

LOTTIE. Poor little thing. So why are you keen on it?

VERA. Well, not a lot people know this, 'cuz they're keeping it real hush-hush, but there's a big role in it for a lady's maid, Tilly. A real good honest-to-God part.

LOTTIE. So, why don't ya ask that white hussy of yours to put a word in for you?

VERA. Gloria? It ain't worth the trouble.

LOTTIE. If it was up to me, I'd —

VERA. Well, it ain't!

LOTTIE. Don't get all bent outta shape. How come I ain't heard nothing about it 'til now?

VERA. I thought you'd given up acting.

LOTTIE. Nonsense. Acting gave up on me.

VERA. Hell, folks've been lining up at Charles Beecher's casting since last week. I swear it. I've been trying to get an audition for days. But he won't see me, he still thinks t'was me that spread the rumor about him and Beth Ann.

LOTTIE. Well, didn't ya?

VERA. Yeah, I did. So what? He had it coming.

LOTTIE. You can say that again, Beecher don't send you out on nothing unless you give 'em a blowjob and twenty-five dollars. And I ain't giving that jackass twenty five dollars to do the same thing he doing for me right now, a whole lotta nothing.

VERA. You better give 'em that twenty-five dollars.

LOTTIE. Why? So he can buy his mistress another pair of alligator shoes? No, thank you.

VERA. Well, sugar, there's work to be had. W-O-R-K! You hear what I'm saying, WORK! Every tap-dancing fool and two-bit hustler's been talking about it … wake up, honey.

LOTTIE. Yeah, yeah. I believe it when I see it. How many times have I heard that damn refrain?

VERA. Turn up your nose, but I'll put it this way, a couple of the Negroes actually get to say something other than yes'um and no'um.

LOTTIE. Seriously? Ya lying! You count the lines?

VERA. Whatcha think?

LOTTIE. And?

VERA. Got tired of counting.

LOTTIE. Get outta here!

VERA. And … Gloria says, they wanna make a discovery.

LOTTIE. Shucks, honey, they ain't even gonna consider nobody like you or me. We been here too long to be discovered.

VERA. Yeah, how do you know?

LOTTIE. How do I know? How do I know? You think I came all the way out to Cali to sew labels into cheap shirts? Darling, I was in the Broadway hit *Suzie Jane*, Kay East called me the best damn shimmier in all of New York City. I did *Blackbirds* with Doris Mills, the engagement at the Alhambra. Went on for her four times. *(Sings, birdlike.)*

I'm a little blackbird looking for a bluebird
You're a little blackbird, get a little lonesome too.

VERA. You were in *Blackbirds*?

LOTTIE. May God strike me down. Shucks, I played Juliet for a group of Pullman porters in Chicago, and received no less than two marriage proposals on closing night. You may not believe this, but I had a slender pretty figure when I first come out here. Yes, indeed. Had to fight off the fellas. Fight 'em like ole Jake Jefferson. But you gotta be high yella mellow or look like you crawled outta Mississippi cotton patch to get work in this rotten town. So here I am, or should I say here I is, seven years later trying to eat my way into some work, looking like someone's mammy and the closest I've gotten to the pictures is sitting in the back row of the cinema.

VERA. You played Juliet?

LOTTIE. I played the hell out of her. You ain't seen a death scene until you've seen this bitch die on stage.

O happy dagger! This is thy sheath;
(Lottie pretends to thrust a dagger into her stomach.)
… there rust, and let me die.
(Lottie drops to the ground. Vera applauds.)

VERA. Bravo! *(Lottie takes a glorious stage bow.)*

LOTTIE. Thank you, thank you, sugar, but that ain't nothing, I got plenty more of that in my pocket. But I'll tell you what, I don't expect this business to hand me anything. 'Cuz only a fool keeps going back to the same well once it's run dry.

VERA. Well, as long as they're casting fools I guess you can count me in.

LOTTIE. "Oh shucks bozz, I'z dun furgots my brain. Lawd haf mercy."

VERA. Oh shut up. You know, you do that far too well.

LOTTIE. *(Seriously.)* Really? You think so? You think I could get work?

VERA. Wherefore art thou, Juliet?!

LOTTIE. Yeah, well, make all the noise you want, but I do recollect somebody saying they wasn't gonna throw on a headrag and play slave.

VERA. C'mon, you know me, honey. Be honest, what if someone put a script in front of you, and you read a role and you knew that role could, well, change your life.

LOTTIE. Ain't no role out there gonna make the sun rise and set. Tell it to a half-dozen smart lookers who came out here thinking they was sweeter than Christmas and now they're getting exercise holding a cup out like the rest of us. *(Lottie gives Vera a "get real" look.)*

VERA. I ain't the only one who spent my last dime to get out here thinking, maybe, just maybe, times was ready to change.

LOTTIE. Well, I ain't gonna argue with you no more, but "Take no more on your heels than you can kick off with your toes," that's what my Mama used to say.

VERA. Do what you want, but I ain't gonna sit around twiddling my thumbs hoping someone'll discover me sleeping on a streetcar. *(Vera exits. Lottie quickly races to the doorway, checking to make sure Vera is gone. Lottie transforms, she is suddenly an "actress" on the stage. She dramatically crosses to find her light and prepares for her death scene.)*

Scene 3

Studio back lot.

Vera, dressed to impress, impatiently rolls a cigarette between her fingers, as she anxiously paces back and forth with a script in her other hand.

Leroy, sharply dressed in an elegant black suit, enters and studies her from afar before deciding whether to approach her. He swings his hat behind his back.

Vera stops.

VERA. "Miss Marie. Miss Marie. Talk to me. Miss Marie."

LEROY. Excuse me, ain't you...? *(Vera stops short, surprised.)*

VERA. *(Lighting up.)* Who?

LEROY. I'm sorry, I guess I'm wrong. For a second you looked like ...

VERA. Who?

LEROY. Oh no, never mind. *(Leroy, playfully, turns to leave. Vera smiles and returns to reading.)* But you know, from a distance, you sure does look like —

VERA. A woman who is about to grow real impatient. Are you trying to flirt with me?

LEROY. Yes, ma'am. I believe I am.

VERA. *(Self-consciously.)* Oh, hiya.

LEROY. Hiya. *(A moment.)* Say, whatcha doing out here all lonesome? Huh? You auditioning for this here New Orleans picture like everyone and their mama?

VERA. Me? Nah. But hell, I'd sure like to. I ... I'm just here working for Gloria Mitchell.

LEROY. Gloria Mitchell?!

VERA. The one and only. She's inside testing for the lead of *The Belle of New Orleans.*

LEROY. No kidding.

VERA. Yeah? Second time this week. She's all nerves and worries. I had the feeling she was about to yell at somebody, and that somebody wasn't going to be me. So I slipped out. Shhh, don't tell anyone I'm back here.

LEROY. *(Whispered.)* No, ma'am. I won't.

VERA. I figure I've got another twenty minutes before she realizes I'm gone, and all hell breaks loose. *(She flirtatiously gives him the once-over.)* Say, will you give me a light?

LEROY. Yes, ma'am.

VERA. Enough with the ma'am. *(Leroy lights Vera's cigarette.)* This ain't Alabama, and I ain't your mama.

LEROY. *(Flirtatiously.)* No, you ain't my mama. *(Savoring.)* Mmmm-hmmm. You're funny.

VERA. Oh, yeah, ha-ha. *(Leroy hums a playful melody.)* What?

LEROY. I know a little somethin'-somethin' about you.

VERA. Do ya now?

LEROY. Yup! You got youself some spirit.

VERA. And you can tell all of that from the way I blow smoke?

LEROY. No. I've been watching you from over there. My buddy, he said this country boy couldn't talk to you. He said you'd chew me up and spit me out. But I told him, I taste too good.

VERA. You know, you were doing swell right up until then.

LEROY. Really? Then I'll take two steps back. *(He takes two sliding steps back.)* There. My name's Leroy Barksdale, I thought I'd let you know before you spit me out. Leroy, that means "the king" in French.

VERA. I'm Vera Stark, which means my parents weren't particularly creative and simply named me after my grandmama.

LEROY. It's my pleasure, Miss Stark.

VERA. So, whatcha doing at the studio in the middle of the day wearing a suit fit for the Ritz?

LEROY. You like? *(Leroy makes a show of his suit.)*

VERA. What ain't to like? Swell threads, polished shoes. I'm guessing you ain't the regular help and I know they don't let sporting Negroes nowhere near the gate. What's your game?

LEROY. Well, as a matter of fact, I work for Maxmillian Von Oster. The director of that there picture.

VERA. That's a lot of name, should I be impressed?

LEROY. Only if those sort of things impress you.

VERA. And what, pray tell, do you do for Mr. Von Oster, other than standing around looking rather high-hat?

LEROY. *(Boastful.)* I'm his Man Friday.

VERA. Well, la di da. Man Friday. Can you get me an audition?

LEROY. … Maybe, what's in it for me?

VERA. You're a fresh one, ain't ya. I betcha some tramps might bite, not this one. *(Leroy straightens his collar, smiles. Pride.)*

LEROY. Whoa. Easy does it.

VERA. You don't look like a Man Friday.

LEROY. No? I'm actually just doing this here thing until I finish night school. *(Proudly.)* I'm a // musician —

VERA. Musician! You and every fella. Yeah, let me guess, you play the saxophone.

LEROY. *(Meant to impress.)* Nope. I play the trumpet, and … I'm studying music theory and composition at the university.

VERA. Music theory? Is that a fancy way of saying you're studying to be a music teacher?

LEROY. No, ma'am, I ain't so interested in teaching, dig. I want to be a composer, you know, write music.

VERA. Yeah, I know what a composer does.

LEROY. 'Cuz that's the only way to make your mark. We got all these great musicians, play their asses off, but half of 'em can't read or write music. Hell, I've been in joints where cats have played the craziest tunes, you know, shook a place right down to its bones, and then the next day can't whistle twelve bars of it 'cuz the gin dun fogged their memory. Do you know "The Saint Louis Blues"?

VERA. Who don't?

LEROY. Yeah, but do you know "The Texas Jaunt"? "See Ya Later, Honey"? *(Leroy beats out a fancy rhythm on his body.)* How about "Hot Memphis Babydoll"? *(Leroy beats out a rhythm on his body, upping the ante. He throws in a whistle or hums a playful melody.)*

VERA. I can't say that I do.

LEROY. Well, there you go. Those are some of the best dang tunes I've ever heard! But you ain't gonna hear 'em, 'cuz a brilliant cat called Clyde "Li'l Bro" Wilson sure can put a hurtin' on the piano, but can't do nothing with a pen and paper. Listen here, my father was a farmer, and if it rained today, it was all right with him. Never was thinking about the future, wasn't thinking about how to stretch his resources a little further, or how to improve for the next year, no ma'am, he'd say hallelujah if something green grew each season. And you see miss, I ain't going to end up bent and penniless like my pops, trying to coax a dollar from land that ain't produced nothing but misery. I'm thinking four – five years ahead of the next cat.

VERA. You one of those new Negroes.

LEROY. Suppose you can say that.

VERA. How come in Los Angeles, nobody actually does what they do? And everybody's always on their way to something else. Something grander.

LEROY. And I suppose you ain't?

VERA. Who said I ain't? I'm just making a friendly observation.

LEROY. And what does Miss Vera Stark do?

VERA. *(Proudly.)* I'm an actress.

LEROY. Oh I see, and so what's the role you're playing today? Gloria Mitchell's maid.

VERA. Ease up, jockey. Don't get too fresh. I am an actress. *(Vera turns away from him. He checks her out from behind.)*

LEROY. So tell me, Miss Stark the actress, what might I have seen you in?

VERA. I've been in quite a few pictures, Man Friday. Have you seen *Shout Amen*?

LEROY. Yes.

VERA. I'm a reveler in the juke joint scene, I'm the gal dancing with gay abandon.

LEROY. That was you?

VERA. So, you remember me?

LEROY. I don't actually, but I'm glad that I saw the picture. I'll remember it more fondly from now on. *(Vera produces a smile.)* And supposin' I could get you an audition?

VERA. *(Eagerly.)* Could ya really?

LEROY. Maybe. Is it a good part? *(Vera smiles.)*

VERA. Oh, I don't know, could be. Tilly, a slave gal who takes care of her ailing mistress 'til the end.

LEROY. Oh, that's original.

VERA. I sense judgment in your voice. Are you one of those people who think the pictures are a blight on our culture? Are you a race man?

LEROY. I like a good picture. *(Leroy does a spot-on impression of Stepin Fetchit. Vera succumbs to laughter.)*

VERA. You're a real fool, man Friday.

LEROY. You find that funny, do ya? Don't get me wrong, I'm up for a good laugh as much as the next fella, but why we still playing slaves? Shucks, it was hard enough getting free the first damn time.

VERA. It's steady work and it beats picking cotton. *(Flirtatiously.)* Did you come all the way across the parking lot to school me?

LEROY. No, ma'am, you seem like a plenty smart gal. And, you're about the prettiest thing I ever seen. And I hope I ain't speaking out of turn, but you don't seem like the sorta gal who'd just stand around back waiting on small opportunities. You seem like the one folks should be paying money to see. If you know what I'm saying.

VERA. I don't know exactly what you're saying, and I don't know you well enough to wanna know what you mean. So let's just agree that we all find creative ways to pay the rent. Excuse me, I better go inside.

LEROY. Hey, hey sister, don't run off. "Ambition should be made of sterner stuff." *(Vera stops herself and smiles.)*

VERA. *Julius Caesar.*

LEROY. I know a thing or two.

VERA. I guess you do. You got my attention. But your thorns need trimming.

LEROY. Where can one find Miss Vera Stark on a Saturday evening?

VERA. Once you figure that out, give me a holler. In the meantime, tend to your garden. *(Vera smiles to herself and exits.)*

Scene 4

Gloria's living room.

Gloria, dressed in a glamorous red evening gown, rushes in with a decorative vase filled with azaleas. She sets them on the coffee table, then frantically searches the bar area.

GLORIA. *(Panicked.)* Vera! Vera! Vera! *(She's growing increasingly panicked, recklessly pulling things from the bar. Vera enters, unseen by Gloria, wearing an elaborate maid's uniform. She silently watches Gloria.)* Vera! VERA! VERA! *(Then —)*

VERA. Gloria, what are you doing?

GLORIA. Oh my God, there you are!

VERA. Have you lost your mind?

GLORIA. He wants bourbon!

VERA. We don't have bourbon, honey.

GLORIA. I know we don't have bourbon! But, he wants bourbon. What are we going to do?

VERA. Tell him we don't have it, and offer him something else.

GLORIA. Bite your tongue! That man out there is the head of the studio! The studio, do you hear me? So, Vera Stark, you find me a bottle of bourbon or so help me I will —

VERA. What?! *(Gloria crumbles.)*

GLORIA. Oh god. This is such a disaster. He's not going to give me this role. I can feel it. He's sitting out there making his decision. Deciding.

VERA. Pull yourself // together.

GLORIA. I tried to call you. I needed you, I was drowning out there.

VERA. Okay. Okay. Calm yourself. *(Vera digs under the couch and produces a bottle of gin.)* Here.

GLORIA. What's that?

VERA. Your special emergency reserve. The good gin.

GLORIA. You wicked woman, that's where you've been hiding it. Give it to me! *(Gloria snatches the bottle. She pours herself an overly generous drink.)* It's just a little drinkie-poo to soften the lighting.

25

(She knocks back the drink.) What? He can't see me drinking. I'm "Gloria Mitchell, America's Little Sweetie Pie." *(Gloria forces a smile and pours herself another healthy-sized drink, and knocks it back. Vera raises her eyebrows.)* Ah, that's better. I almost feel myself. Okay, now what am I doing?

VERA. You'll make him one of your special martinis.

GLORIA. Of course, I will! Thank you. I adore you. *(Gloria goes about making Slasvick a martini. Vera lifts up the flowers.)*

VERA. I put these azaleas on the table. Why are they back here?

GLORIA. I moved them, the colors were rather assertive. I was beginning to feel a bit upstaged, couldn't they have come in a more subtle color?

VERA. Well, next time I'll ask God to be more accommodating. *(Gloria starts to leave with the martini, then abruptly changes her mind.)*

GLORIA. I can't go back out there. I've run out of conversation. It's awful, Vera. I went deep into my reservoir, and you know it doesn't go very deep. I can't do it —

VERA. Honey, you know your problem, you don't realize how damn lucky you are. Mr. Slasvick's out there for the taking and with a little flutter of your eyelashes you can have everything you want.

GLORIA. *(Dismissively.)* Oh bother, you don't know how much work this takes. It's exhausting to be this fabulous.

VERA. Then shove over, sister, and let someone else do it for a change. I've had to bite into a lot of sour apples since I've been out here, and you don't hear me complaining. *(Vera holds out the bowl of chocolates to her.)* But go on, eat your heart out. Dive off Mount Olympus and join the rest of us. *(Gloria is tempted to take one. She fights the impulse.)*

GLORIA. Oh, throw them away! You witch! Why are you trying to ruin me? *(She suddenly has a fresh, brilliant idea.)* I'm going to change. It's all wrong, this dress is all wrong. *(Gloria makes a show shedding her sheer silky shawl.)*

VERA. Oh, quit your yapping. You're not changing. You look stunning.

GLORIA. Really? Do I? *(Gloria finds her perfect lighting, and strikes a glamorous pose.)*

VERA. Oh, brother. *(Lottie enters, also in an elaborate maid's uniform, carrying a bucket of ice and sliced lemons. Lottie goes about setting up the bar.)* Get back out there before that man leaves. *(Gloria, tipsy, starts to leave, then notices Lottie.)*

GLORIA. Excuse me? And who are you?!

LOTTIE. I'm —

GLORIA. Vera, why is this strange woman staring at me?

VERA. It's Lottie, my roommate, Lottie, you hired her to help out tonight.

GLORIA. Of course I did! Why are you confusing me? This is a very important evening for me! *(Gloria exits in a flurry with the martini.)*

LOTTIE. Oh dear Lord, someone bring common sense back into this world.

VERA. C'mon, help me fluff these pillows and then we'll bring the rest of the food out to the patio. *(Vera carries the chocolates.)*

LOTTIE. Hey, hey, hold on there just a minute. *(Lottie takes a handful of chocolates.)* No reason for 'em to go to waste. *(Vera tosses the rest of the chocolates in a wastebasket.)* And honey, I'm gonna need a little taste of something to get me through this mess. Where's the good stuff? *(Vera goes to the liquor cabinet and pours each of them a drink.)*

VERA. May we survive this evening, cheers! *(Lottie and Vera knock back their drinks. Lottie rips off the maid's hat.)*

LOTTIE. And for the record, I ain't wearing this idiotic thing. I ain't gonna. I don't care what she says. *(Imitating Gloria.)* Vera, Vera, Vera, oh there you are, I've lost my mind and I can't find it anywhere. Help me, oh please help me. *(Vera throws a pillow at Lottie.)*

VERA. Oh, stop it. C'mon, give me a hand. *(Vera and Lottie go about fluffing the couch pillows.)*

LOTTIE. Satin? Boy, this is some swell joint.

VERA. Ain't it though.

LOTTIE. Even the booze taste better here. Who knew? Yeah, I could definitely get used to this.

VERA. Dream on.

LOTTIE. Honey, you don't know how hard I'm dreaming right now. *(Lottie whistles. Gloria reenters like a gust of wind. She carries an empty plate. Lottie pretends to be busy.)*

GLORIA. Oh, I practically forgot to mention, it appears we'll have two more this evening. The little prick took the liberty of inviting the director Maxmillian Von Oster to join us for dessert, sugar. Isn't that glorious? The director of *The Belle of New Orleans* is going to be here! *(Vera and Lottie grow excited.)*

VERA. Really?

GLORIA. *(To Lottie.)* And why are you standing around doing nothing? We need more salami. *(Gloria exits in a flourish.)*

VERA. Two more, I'm afraid I won't have enough for —

LOTTIE. Who cares? After a couple martinis they won't hardly notice. But honey, did you hear what she said? The director of *The Belle of New Orleans* is coming here. The director.

VERA. Yeah, and?

LOTTIE. And, and, and? *(Sings.)*

   Tell ole Pharaoh, let my peoples goooo

(On "go," Lottie slowly and dramatically puts back on the maid's cap, and exits singing. Vera smiles and picks up Gloria's shawl. She theatrically drapes it around her shoulders.)

VERA. Darling, of course I'd love to be in your picture, do I sing? Why, of course, I do. *(She dramatically crosses the room and finds her light. She begins to sing a song like "Gimme a Pigfoot (and a Bottle of Beer)."* She does a sexy dance. Mr. Slasvick enters and stands in the doorway, watching Vera. Mr. Slasvick applauds. She is startled by his presence and stops singing —)* Oh, shit. I'm sorry. Would you like something more, sir?

SLASVICK. That is a question I often ask myself.

VERA. I mean —

SLASVICK. I know what you mean. Yes, give me a pig foot and a bottle of beer. No, no, actually I'll have a seltzer with a lime. *(Vera goes about pouring Slasvick a seltzer. Mr. Slasvick rubs his stomach.)*

VERA. Is something wrong, sir?

SLASVICK. I don't particularly enjoy these gatherings. Somehow they always manage to upset my stomach. So if you don't mind, I'm going to grab a bit of quiet before anyone notices I'm gone.

VERA. No problem, the chair over there is comfortable. It's my personal favorite.

SLASVICK. Thank you. *(Slasvick sits.)* What's your name?

VERA. Mine? Vera.

SLASVICK. Vera, you're a very pretty colored girl.

VERA. I suppose I should say thank you.

SLASVICK. I don't want you to think me forward, but it's my job to notice these things. You ever thought about being in pictures?

VERA. Yes, sir, who in this town ain't.

SLASVICK. Vera. Means faith in my language. Do you have a last name?

VERA. Stark.

---

* See Special Note on Songs and Recordings on copyright page.

SLASVICK. Vera Stark, sounds like a name our publicity department would've cooked up. Vera Stark. "Vera Stark." I like, maybe we'll borrow it.

VERA. I ain't loaning out my name, I hope to do something with it one day.

SLASVICK. Good for you, Vera. If you find something good in this rotten business, hold onto it. *(Gloria, exasperated, enters, she doesn't notice Mr. Slasvick.)*

GLORIA. Oh God, quick, quick, I need a drink and something to eat. I've been sucking in my stomach for over an hour, so that pompous little prick won't notice that — *(Vera clears her throat to silently alert Gloria of Slasvick's presence. Gloria catches herself, and shifts into "Sweetie Pie" mode.)* Darling, would you be so kind as to pour me another glass of lemonade. I'm simply parched. *(Vera gives Gloria a look and pours her lemonade. Feigns surprise.)* Oh, Mr. Slasvick, I didn't realize you were hiding there. You're missing all of the fun. Really. *(Affecting innocence.)* Sammy Welsh was telling the gang all about his trip to Puerto Rico, did you know that they have cockfighting in Puerto Rico, cockfighting, can you imagine? Grown men … cockfighting. Really.

SLASVICK. *(Sarcastically.)* I'm sorry I missed all that fun?

GLORIA. Up, up, I won't have you sitting here all by yourself. *(Gloria pulls a reluctant Slasvick from his chair. He resists. The doorbell rings. Excited.)* Oh, I wonder who that could be? *(Slasvick, relieved, retreats to the chair.)* Vera. The door. Vera!

VERA. Pipe down, I hear ya. *(Gloria finds her light and strategically strikes a dramatic pose. Vera answers the door. Maxmillian Von Oster, an exquisitely haughty man, enters with Anna Mae — who wears Vera's coat — on his arm. They make a grand entrance. Vera is shocked to find her roommate standing in the doorway.)*

GLORIA. *(Dramatically.)* Maxmillian! *(Gloria makes a dramatic cross.)*

MAX. Gloria, you look radiant.

GLORIA. Thank you, just a little something I threw on. And who is this … lovely creature?

MAX. Allow me to introduce Miss Anna Maria Fernandez of Rio de Janiero. *(Gloria jealously gives Anne Mae the once-over. Anna Mae gives Vera a "please don't expose me" plea with her eyes.)*

GLORIA. Gloria Mitchell, charmed. *(Anna Mae has cobbled together a Brazilian accent.)*

ANNA MAE. I can' believe I'm actually meetin' America's Lettle Sweetie Pie.

GLORIA. *(Sourly.)* In the flesh.

SLASVICK. Von Oster.

MAX. My friend.

SLASVICK. Your timing is impeccable. I'm glad you made it.

MAX. My lovely Anna insisted. I vanted her to meet you. I think our Anna has very great potential. *(Anna Mae strikes her most glamorous pose. Anna Mae extends her hand to Mr. Slasvick. He kisses it.)*

VERA. *(Under her breath.)* Oh brother!

SLASVICK. My pleasure.

ANNA MAE. *(Flirtatiously.)* De pleasure es mine. *(Gloria, irritated by the performance, breaks in.)*

GLORIA. Enough of that, won't you come in and make yourself comfortable.

ANNA MAE. *(With accent.)* Jou 'ave a beautiful home. Ain't it beautiful, Maxie?

MAX. Yes, my love.

GLORIA. Thank you. Don't just stand there looking so formal, come on in, get a drink. *(Vera, dumbstruck, doesn't move.)* Vera! Vera, will you please take Miss Fernandez's lovely coat.

ANNA MAE. Thank jou. *(Anna Mae holds out the coat. Vera snatches it.)* Careful, we don' wan' it to git rrrinkled.

VERA. Don't you worry, I'm gonna take rrreal good care of it, "Miss Fernandez." *(Vera carefully drapes the coat over a chair. A moment.)*

GLORIA. So honey, what are we drinking? You'll have to catch up with the rest of us heathens.

ANNA MAE. I'll 'ave a gin. Double.

VERA. *(Beneath her breath.)* I'll bet you will.

ANNA MAE. With a twist of limon, *obrigado.*

GLORIA. Maxmillian, darling?

MAX. Same for me.

GLORIA. Gin it is. *(Vera pours the drinks. Anna Mae makes a sexy show of crossing the room, both men follow her with their eyes. The women watch Anna Mae with obvious contempt. Gloria's eyes fall on Anna Mae's butt, as she bends to sit.)* Don't you have the cutest little … accent. I always wanted an … a-ccent, but we have to work with what God gives us, don't we. *(Anna Mae seductively drapes herself across the couch.)*

ANNA MAE. I find dat to be so. I wish I didn't 'ave accent. 'Ere in America, it es difficult because not everyone understands vat I say.

GLORIA. *(A little edge.)* Oh, I understand you perfectly, honey. *(Gloria sucks in her stomach and crosses the room, trying to recapture the attention. She lights a cigarette.)* Cigarette?

SLASVICK. Thank you.

GLORIA. Cigarette?

MAX. Please. *(Gloria makes a show of offering both men cigarettes, deliberately excluding Anna Mae as she reaches for one.)*

ANNA MAE. Maxie vas telling me all about his new picture *De Belle of New Orleans*. It sounds very, very interesting. *(Vera gives Anna Mae a pinch as she serves her a glass.)* Ow!

GLORIA. Yes, we're all quite interested in *The Belle of New Orleans*. I just adore the script, as I've told you, Maxmillian.

MAX. It is a very good script, if I may say so. *(Lottie enters carrying a tray of glasses. She nearly drops it upon seeing Anna Mae. Shoots her "be quiet" look.)*

LOTTIE. *(Aside to Vera.)* What's she doing here?

VERA. Digging for gold.

LOTTIE. *(Whispered.)* You gotta be kidding.

VERA. Do I look like I'm laughing? *(Anna Mae gives Lottie a triumphant smile.)*

ANNA MAE. Tell dem what jou told me, Maxie.

MAX. It is my plan to film on location in New Orleans. In brothel. I want the grittiness and sensuality of the place to be palpable.

ANNA MAE. Ain't that exciting!?

MAX. It is so hard to capture flavors, the true essence of city like New Orleans, on studio back lot. Am I correct in saying so? The quality of light in the South, I find it so, so fantastic. It is different from the crisp cold skies of California. It is moist, thick, viscous. I vant that, because of course how I position actors in the environment will inform or perhaps transform their very performance. Indeed! I vant heat.

GLORIA. It sounds thrilling!

SLASVICK. It sounds expensive.

MAX. Of course it is, that is the point, we vant it to be spectacular. Fresh. We vant it to feel thoroughly authentic. If *The Belle of New Orleans* is like every other film that we've seen, then vhat is the point. It is time for cinema to take bold new leap. It is time to capture the truth. For instance, I vant the Negroes to be real, to be Negroes of the earth, I vant to feel their struggle, the rhythm of their language, I vant actors that … no, I don't vant actors, I vant people. *(Vera and Lottie slowly shift their posture, auditioning for the roles of slaves.)* Negroes who have felt the burden of hard unmerciful labor. *(Vera and Lottie continue to morph into slave women.)* I vant to see hundred years of oppression in the hunch of their shoulders. *(Vera and Lottie hunch their shoulders, continuing to morph. Vera, seeing an opportunity, slowly and in the character of a slave, crosses to freshen his drink, her gait slow, posture deferential.)*

VERA. Suh, you want another drink, suh?

MAX. Yes! Thank you! *(Ecstatic.)* I vant to hear the music of the fields. The songs of strife and struggle. *(Lottie begins to softly hum a spiritual. Vera joins in.)* Yes, that is the sound. *(To Vera.)* Where are you from, my dear? *(A moment.)*

VERA. Me, suh?

MAX. What's your tragic story? *(Vera looks to Gloria, and makes a decision.)*

VERA. I … I … um, wuz born in the Mississippi Delta, but I was raised just outside of New Orleans.

MAX. Yes, vonderful. *(Lottie continues to hum, underscoring Vera's story.)*

VERA. *(Lying.)* My mama died in childbirth 'cuz there wasn't no doctor there to birth me proper, and you see my pappy wuz a blues man, and he guitar was the onliest thing he luv. My pappy dun own heself a juke joint. And as a chil' I work-did dere 'cuz he couldn' afford no other help. Nah, suh. I work-did like a grown woman, though I was nuthin' but a chil'. I dun seen plenty of ugly things, things no chil' need see. But my pappy was a good man, but mister, sometime in de South, a good man hafta do ugly things just to survive. *(Maxmillian closes his eyes, savoring. Anna Mae rolls her eyes.)*

MAX. … Sing something, I vant to hear the blues.

GLORIA. *(Wickedly.)* Yes, go on, Vera. Sing us the blues, because you know them so well. *(A moment. Vera realizes she's out of her depth. She launches into an improvised song. Lottie provides vocal bluesy punctuation.)*

VERA. *(Discovering.)*

    My man he dun treat me wrong,

    I said, my man he dun treat me wrong,

    He a low-down dirty bastard.

but hell if our love ain't strong.

My man he mean and nasty —

LOTTIE. Nasty!

VERA. But he ... he ... *(Tears well up in Vera's eyes. She's giving a performance of a lifetime.)* I can't, no, it too painful. It dun take me home, and home ain't someplace dat so easy to be.

MAX. Yes, I understand. As child I fled Cossacks, but still for me Russia is home. But even now it vould be too painful to recall bittersweet music of home. You see, Fredrick. This is what we need on the screen. Authenticity. Just as Anna Maria conjures the flavors of carnivale in Brazil. This broken Negro woman, her sad mournful face, the coarse rhythm of her language, tells the story of the South. *(Vera manages a slight broken smile. Gloria, suddenly feeling upstaged, interjects.)*

GLORIA. *(With Southern accent.)* Yes, sugar, but how do you see the little ole role of Marie, the octoroon?

MAX. She has lived life!

GLORIA. *(With Southern accent.)* Yes, of course. That's wonderful, sugar.

MAX. I vant the lines and the creases in the faces of the prostitutes in my brothel to tell their story.

SLASVICK. Whores? I didn't realize that there were any whores in the script.

MAX. It is set in brothel.

SLASVICK. Yes, but it doesn't mean they need to be ... whores. Couldn't we make them something else, something less objectionable?

MAX. Like?

SLASVICK. I don't know, something less, prostitutey, but equally distasteful like a, a night club singer or ... or an actress. Von Oster, I want to be clear, we can't have whores, not as long as the studio is making this picture. When you came to me with a book about a slave woman in New Orleans, I didn't balk, I said let's do it, I was even willing to keep the lead as an octoroon, as long as she's played by a white woman and there's no mention that she's colored. I don't wanna make a federal case out of this, but, but if our lead is a whore and we have a bunch of Negroes running around selling misery, we won't even be able to open the picture in New York City.

MAX. That is little detail. It is the truth that I'm after.

SLASVICK. Fuck the truth, I signed on for a romance with pretty gals in corsets and hoop skirts.

MAX. You will have it all.

SLASVICK. Well, I don't want it all, that's what I'm worried about. *(To Vera.)* Vera, could I have some bicarbonate soda, please.

VERA. *(In character.)* Yes, suh!

ANNA MAE. And little freshen for me too! *(Anna Mae holds out her glass, Vera ignores her.)*

MAX. I must have freedom!

SLASVICK. When you own the studio, you can buy your own damn freedom. Until then no whores, no cotton pickin' slaves, no misery. I want romance, and maybe a couple of musical numbers. If I wanted a critique of antebellum New Orleans, I'd have checked a book out of the library. Look here, Von Oster, there is a fucking Depression, people are lining up at soup kitchens, mothers are selling their babies, nobody wants to hear the blues ...

ANNA MAE. *(Blurts.)* I love de blues.

MAX. You see that! People vant the truth. They vant real life, like this woman here. Vhat is your name?

VERA. Vera, suh.

MAX. You see, she is not actress, she is woman who wears her miserable life like blossom about to flower and it is beautiful. And vhy can't we celebrate that beauty on the screen?

SLASVICK. People want to laugh, they want to cry and they want a little song and dance in between. And I don't think that's so fucking awful. But the one thing they don't want is to feel bad about themselves. Not now, not while the economy is dying and good folks are being forced out of their homes and into the fucking gutter. People need the past, need their history to seem heroic, glorious and romantic. That is what we do, erase their pain for ninety minutes. And let's face it, slavery ain't exactly a pick-me-up. All I'm asking is that if you're gonna give 'em slaves, give 'em happy ones. *(Vera and Lottie let out involuntary gasps of surprise.)*

MAX. I am director! Do you vant me to make something beautiful, truthful, elegant or do you vant the shit that you pull from the asses of imbeciles? Tell me now, right here! Don't waste my time. I demand to know! Right now! I vant answer!

SLASVICK. I want romance! There's my fucking answer.

MAX. I love this script, and I von't be told vhat to do! *(Maximillian storms out of the room.)*

SLASVICK. Don't you walk away from me! This conversation isn't over. I run this goddamn studio! *(Mr. Slasvick storms off in a huff.)*

GLORIA. Okie dokie. A little difference of opinion. I better go and make sure no one falls into the pool. *(Gloria starts to exit and then stops herself.)* Oh Vera, next time you want to play a scene, perhaps you could let your scene partners know ahead of time. *(Gloria exits. A moment.)*

LOTTIE. I'm gonna go hide in the kitchen. *(Lottie gives Anna Mae a kick and exits. Vera stares at Anna Mae.)*

ANNA MAE. *(Sings.)*

Camptown ladies sing dis song, doo-dah! doo-dah!

Camptown racetrack five miles long, oh, doo-dah day —

VERA. Oh shut up!

ANNA MAE. You heard the man he's looking for happy slaves.

VERA. Then I suppose you're perfect for the part.

ANNA MAE. What happened to my drink? *(Anna Mae holds out her drink.)*

VERA. Get your own damn drink.

ANNA MAE. Yes'um. *(Anna Mae goes to the bar, and pours herself a healthy drink.)*

VERA. You're playing way out of your league, honey.

ANNA MAE. Ain't I though, it's only 'cuz my playmates don't care for the games I play.

VERA. How long do you think you can keep up the front?

ANNA MAE. Oh, he's buying what I'm selling, even if it ain't the real thing. Trust me, in the bedroom, a horny joe ain't so particular about the accent.

VERA. You are one devious dame.

ANNA MAE. Oh, grow up, everyone in this town has an angle. Listen here, I'm gonna get me a role in this picture, and the studio ain't gonna have a whole lot to say about it. *(Anna Mae belts back her cocktail.)*

VERA. Whoa, ain't you getting a little ahead of yourself. *(Lottie enters with Leroy in tow.)*

LOTTIE. Found this one hanging at the back door of the kitchen, you know 'em? Says he's the chauffeur. *(Vera's surprised.)*

LEROY. Vera Stark! I've been leaving messages for you all around town.

VERA. What did you do with Von Oster's man Friday?

LEROY. Well —

VERA. The hat's a nice touch.

LEROY. It's kinda silly, but you know how it is. *(Leroy, embarrassed, removes the hat.)*

ANNA MAE. Ain't you supposed to be watching the car?

LOTTIE. Ain't you supposed to be colored? *(Lottie bursts into laughter.)*

ANNA MAE. All right, all right, get it outta your system.

LEROY. What did I miss? Does someone wanna share the joke with me?

VERA. Why don't you ask Señorita Fernandez of Rio De Janiero?

ANNA MAE. Ha ha ha. I'm laughing.

LEROY. What happened to your accent?

ANNA MAE. What? Are you gonna tell on me?

LEROY. How about that. I knew it. Hot damn, I knew somethin' was up. *(Leroy's tickled silly.)* You know, 'cuz when you first climbed your ass into the car, you gave me a look, and baby I knew there was some pork fat in that hello. Can't fool me, little sister.

ANNA MAE. So, what's the big deal? Some broads dye their hair blonde. And some of us are a little more "creative." Believe me, I ain't the only colored gal masquerading for a living. Get off my back. *(Imitating Vera.)* Yes, suh, you wants another drink? There you go, suh. *(To Vera.)*

VERA. I es from Rio De Janiero, I no speaky English. *(They do some sexy samba steps.)* Honey, you ain't the only one looking for work.

LOTTIE. Yeah. And some of us field Negroes don't have it so easy.

LEROY. Man, oh man. If Von Oster found out —

ANNA MAE. Well, he ain't gonna. *(Gloria, tipsy and exasperated, reenters.)*

GLORIA. Quick, quick, I need another drink! *(Gloria glares at Anna Mae. The women have a silent showdown.)*

ANNA MAE. *(With accent.)* Desculpe-me, I better go check on Maxie.

GLORIA. You do that. *(Anna Mae exits in a hurry.)*

VERA. How's it going?

GLORIA. This is a disaster! Something has to be done or this picture isn't going to happen, and it has to happen. I need it to fucking happen! *(She notices Leroy, and pulls herself together. Flirtatiously.)* Who's this?

LEROY. Leroy Barksdale, I drive for Mr. Von Oster, ma'am.

GLORIA. Is it a big car? *(She's outwardly seductive with him.)*

LEROY. Yes, ma'am.

VERA. Oh brother!

GLORIA. How come every time I come into my living room I find someone new standing there? It's like a rent party in Harlem, where people just show up, drink your booze and pretend like they're lending you a hand.

LEROY. What do you know about rent parties in Harlem?

GLORIA. *(Lying.)* Absolutely nothing. *(Gloria giggles, as if remembering something wonderful.)*

VERA. That's the official story. *(She is completely liquored up.)*

GLORIA. If you need me, I'll be in my bedroom slitting my wrists.

VERA. Okay. *(Gloria slyly beckons Leroy to follow, then drunkenly exits.)*

LEROY. That's America's Sweetie Pie?

VERA. Welcome to the house of mirrors, if you can find your way out of here, good luck.

LEROY. I ain't leaving just yet. It seems to me the real fun's just beginning.

VERA. Well, I better get out there —

LOTTIE. No, you stay, it's my turn to audition. *(Lottie exits in character. Leroy pours himself a drink, takes a cigarette from the holder.)*

VERA. *(Sarcastically.)* Make yourself comfortable, why don't ya.

LEROY. Don't mind if I do. *(Leroy lights his cigarette and plops back down on the couch.)*

VERA. *(Sarcastically.)* Take off your shoes, I'll run ya bath.

LEROY. Would ya, sugar? *(He flirtatiously reaches out and grabs her arm, pulling her down next to him.)*

VERA. Look here, tonic, I'm on duty. I gotta work. *(Vera stands up.)*

LEROY. Relax, I ain't worried about them white folks. The gin and whiskey's gonna take care of them.

VERA. Easy for you to say, but there's a lot riding on this evening. So have a drink and be your way.

LEROY. It tickles me how half the Negroes in this town are running around like chickens without heads trying to get five minutes of shucking and jiving time, all so they can say they're in the pictures. It's just lights and shadows, what's the big deal? I'm a musician, right? I play cuz' it's like how I tell my story. And I can begin here in chains — *(Leroy hums, whistles, sings and beats out "Dixie," slowly deconstructing the song, transforming it from a simple familiar melody into something entirely fresh, new, complicated and playful. Vera smiles, seduced.)* And I can end right there. Free. If you wanna be in pictures, where you gonna begin, and where are you gonna end? Dig?

VERA. You're one heavy cat. What do you care? It's just lights and shadows, as you say. And I ain't gonna lie, I've been dreaming of the pictures ever since I saw Little Moonglow Willie crack a smile at the ten-cent arcade. I know it's silly, but I've wanted to be up there with Willie, making folks laugh 'til they're stupid. Hell, I've been out here five years chasing after Willie. I've walked my feet raw trying to get a break. Told myself a million times, "It ain't worth it, Vera. Pack your bags, go on home." It's just lights and shadows, right? But, I've been performing since I was six years old. There's nothing I can't do. You want me to do the soft shoe, I'll do it, and I'll do it so good it'll embarrass you. All right, imagine if you had no place to blow your horn.

LEROY. Well, that ain't gonna happen.

VERA. All right then. So you see, I ain't ready to give up just yet. And before you came in here, tonic, I actually did something I vowed I'd never do, and I did it so easily it frightened me. And I got to thinking about what I'd be willing to do to have a taste of what Gloria's got. You know, be a star! And tonight I crossed a bridge, and I'm telling you, I ain't going back!

End of Act One

ACT TWO

Scene 1

The movie. Black and white. The Belle of New Orleans. A richly appointed Southern boudoir, circa 1855.

Gloria, playing the role of sickly Marie, the octoroon mistress of a wealthy merchant, sits up in bed.

Anne Mae, playing the role of Cecilia, a lively French singer and Gloria's best friend, enters laughing.

The acting is the emotionally grand style of the early 1930s. Faces are expressive, movement sharp and theatrical. It shouldn't be a parody, but rather a true attempt to capture the cinematic style of that period. The costumes are sumptuous and playful.

ANNA MAE. *(Playfully, with French accent.)* Marie, what are you still doing in bed? I thought surely you'd be packed and halfway to L'hermitage by now. *(Gloria is weak, she struggles to speak.)*
GLORIA. No. I'm not going. *(Cecilia is shocked by the revelation.)*
ANNA MAE. Not going? But, why? That's all you've been talking about for days.
GLORIA. I can't. I can't marry him. *(Gloria coughs.)*
ANNA MAE. But, why?
GLORIA. There are too many lies between us. If I leave here, Madame Pierre has threatened to tell him the truth, that my blood isn't pure, that it carries a drop of shame and misery. I'm an octoroon, Cecile, and eventually he will discover the truth. *(Dramatic music. Gloria closes her eyes.)*
ANNA MAE. I have the blood of a noble French family, and look at how much good it's done me here in New Orleans. *(Anna Mae takes Gloria's hand.)* He loves you. What does it matter?

GLORIA. Now, but what happens when he finds out that I'm the daughter of a slave woman? Will he still want me to be the mistress of the grand L'hermitage? *(Tears shower Gloria's face.)*

ANNA MAE. Don't cry, Marie. *(Gloria coughs, she tries to get out of bed, but doesn't have the strength.)* What is it?

GLORIA. It's the fever.

ANNA MAE. It will break soon.

GLORIA. No, Cecile, it won't. I'm … I'm dying. *(The music dramatically punctuates her words. Anna Mae covers her mouth, registering shock.)*

ANNA MAE. Oh my poor sweet, Marie. *(Anna Mae feels Gloria's head. Vera Stark as Tilly, a slave girl, stands in the doorway.)*

VERA. Dere you is, Mis' Cecile, Madame Pierre be wanting you yes'erday. She fit to be tied. Now ya's best be gettin' down dere, 'fore she tan ya hide.

ANNA MAE. *(To Marie.)* Rest, I'll be right back shortly.

GLORIA. Don't leave me.

ANNA MAE. Rest. *(Anna Mae leaves. Gloria weeps.)*

VERA. Don't worry, Mis', Tilly gonna take good care of ya. Sho'nuff is. You gonna get through dis' and soon you be back out dere. Madame Grace nearly finish wit' ya gown, and come Friday ya's gonna put it on, and be de prettiest thing dat ever dun danced the quadrille at de Magnolia Ball.

GLORIA. Wouldn't that be lovely. *(Vera has something urgent to say, but is hesitant to share it. She goes to the door, then reconsiders.)* What is it, Tilly? Tell me.

VERA. *(Hesitantly.)* Mis', Mr. Lafayette here to see ya. *(Gloria registers shock and dismay.)*

GLORIA. Tell him I'm not here. I can't bear to face him, not like this, not now, not after all that has happened.

VERA. But, he already know ya's here. Dat rascal Cassius dun tol' him.

GLORIA. Tell him to go. Tell him I'm sleeping. Tell him anything. No, I can't. No. No. I don't want to see him.

VERA. He ain't want me to say, but he missing ya sum'ting awful —

GLORIA. Oh, won't you tell him to go already! *(Vera reluctantly turns to leave.)* Wait. *(Tenderly.)* Does he look well?

VERA. He look real good, Mis'. *(Gloria smiles, wrestling with what to say.)*

GLORIA. Did he bring azaleas?

VERA. Ya know he always do. *(Gloria gasps dramatically.)*

GLORIA. And does he know? Did you tell him I'm dying? *(Gloria coughs, she grows faint.)*

VERA. I don't know, what he know. But I do know dat he here. Mis', dat man out dere loves ya. And if you send him away now, it gonna be a real shame. Ya can't keep hidin' from de worl'. Talk to him, tell him how ya feel. Tell him ya love him. 'Cause ya and I know dere ain't no other man in ya heart but him.

GLORIA. How do you put up with me? *(Gloria reaches out for Vera's hand.)*

VERA. Mis', whatcha want me to tell him? *(A long dramatic pause. Close-up on Gloria's intense face carrying the dramatic burden of the moment.)*

GLORIA. Tell him to remember me on that warm spring day we went boating on the bayou. I was wearing that violet cardigan that Mammy made. It was a perfect afternoon, as perfect as it could be. And if he remembers, as I do, we didn't ever want it to end. I like to think of us that way. *(Gloria, spent, closes her eyes.)*

VERA. Mis' Marie. Mis' Marie! Talk to me. Mis' Marie. Oh Lawdy, Mis' please don't die on me, you can't leave me, what will Tilly do without her mis'? Ya remember when we wuz younguns running barefoot in the backyard and you dun found dat wounded bird, and Mammy said let it die, but ya ... ya taught dat poor thang to fly again. Well, you dat bird, and I ain't gonna let you go without a fight. Fight! *(Gloria manages to say —)*

GLORIA. I have no more fight, Tilly.

VERA. I ain't gonna let you go. Don't die, Mis', don't die. You the only thing I's got. Mis' Marie. *(Gloria opens her eyes.)*

GLORIA. *(Triumphantly.)* I'm free, Tilly. I'm free. *(Vera's eyes grow large at the notion. She mouths the word, "Free.")*

VERA. Stay awake, and together we'll face a new day. *(Gloria gently touches Vera's face. Vera takes Gloria's hand. Gloria dies. Her hand drops away from Vera's grip. Vera sobs. Anna Mae and Lottie, dressed as a slave woman, enter and stand over the bed.)*

MARIE. Po' Marie.

LOTTIE. She in he'ben now. *(Vera pulls herself up. Music swells. Vera opens the curtains and majestic light fills the boudoir. The movie ends. Lights up on Herb Forrester standing onstage next to the screen. 2003, Hollywood, a colloquium.)*

HERB. I see some new folks have just wandered in. If you're look-

41

ing for the colloquium, "Rediscovering Vera Stark, the Legacy of *The Belle of New Orleans*," you've arrived! If you could quickly take your seats, I have a few brief remarks, before I roll a recently redis-covered clip of Vera Stark's final interview on *The Brad Donovan Show* in 1973. Can I have a little more volume on the mic please? And if you could cue the system. Thank you. *(Stills of Vera Stark in the* Belle of New Orleans *run in the background as he speaks. Herb speaks with deep passion and urgency.)*

HERB. As I was saying, the film is an adaptation of the controver-sial novel *The Belle of New Orleans,* written by Bernard St. Simon in 1852. It tells the story of two slave sisters in New Orleans in the mid-nineteenth century; Marie, the beautiful octoroon prostitute, and Tilly, her devoted servant and companion. Marie is played by Gloria Mitchell, "America's Little Sweetie Pie" and Tilly is played, of course, by Vera Stark in her first major screen appearance. Vera does her best to bring life and complexity to the underwritten role of Tilly, and it's in many ways her performance that elevates the film to ... dare I say it ... art. *(A still of Vera tightening Gloria's corset.)* In the early '30s, Hollywood was beginning to push bound-aries, black folks were cavorting onscreen, women were stripping out of their stockings and exploring their ... sexuality. And thank-fully, *The Belle of New Orleans* was made in this pre-code Hollywood, thus the relationship between the two women onscreen is more tender and textured then anything we'll see between races until the '50s. However, it's ironic that a film that is fundamentally about the politics of race, deliberately goes out of its way to avoid discussing slavery; in fact it's only near the end of the film that we discover Marie's true racial identity. She's an octoroon. Slavery is merely the exotic backdrop. *"Papier peint."* The wall-paper. Indeed, *The Belle of New Orleans* paints a portrait of a romantic and idealized world, where the slave woman Tilly doesn't long for freedom, but merely to please her dying mistress. It's a grotesque misrepresentation of history. So you ask, why? Why? WHY are WE still intrigued by this damn movie! Why are WE still talking about it! Well, it's because Vera Stark's subversive and nuanced performance bears further examination. She is at once in the role and commenting on it. It is a revolutionary performance, dare I say political performance. What was she saying to us? Oh, I see a few standing in the back. Please don't be shy, join us. I didn't mean to go on like this, and in a moment I'll play the recently rediscovered footage from *The Brad Donovan Show*, and as we watch I'd like to plant one question in your heads, what happened to Vera Stark? In late 1973 she mysteriously disappeared. Why? Did she take her own life as it's been suggested in Grandford Ellis' brilliant book *Subverting Blackness*? Or was she cannibalized by our culture? These are questions that have perplexed a generation of American cinephiles. Indeed, controversy plagued Vera's later career, her early promise was … was. But before we get into that, I'd like to introduce our esteemed panelists. Professor of Media and Gender Studies at USVC, Carmen Levy-Green. *(Carmen Levy-Green, a stout and stylish academic, enters and sits.)*

CARMEN. Thank you, it's my pleasure to be here.

HERB. And journalist, poet and performer Afua Assata Ejobo. *(Afua Assata Ejobo, a very hip and slightly masculine woman, enters and sits.)*

AFUA. Thank you, Brother Herb, I'm very excited to be part of this conversation.

HERB. And for those of you who don't know me, I'm Herb Forrester, a filmmaker, musician and entrepreneur from Oakland. Let's, um, roll footage, please. Lights.

Scene 2

1973. The Brad Donovan Show *intro music. Applause. The bright colorful sheen of early seventies television talk show.*

The host, Brad Donovan, sits on the stage next to Peter Rhys-Davies, a groovy English rock musician casually sprawled across a chair. Brad Donovan stands to introduce —

BRAD. She first graced the silver screen in a little film called *The Belle of New Orleans. (Applause.)* Yes. She has had a remarkable career that has spanned over four glorious decades. She's currently headlining in the Folies Bergère at the Tropicana in Las Vegas. My next guest needs little if any introduction. The incomparable Vera Stark. *(Vera Stark in her early 60s, sexy, ebullient and hardened by*

---

* See Special Note on Songs and Recordings on copyright page.

booze, enters, dressed to kill. She makes a grand entrance, ravenously absorbing the applause. She sings a song like "Fly Me to the Moon."* Applause.) The incomparable Vera Stark.

VERA. Thank you, thank you. Isn't he marvelous, and so very, very handsome. *(Applause. They embrace.)*

BRAD. I must ask, because I always do. What on earth are you wearing? Let the audience see.

VERA. *(To studio audience.)* Do you like it?! *(Vera makes an elaborate show of her dress.)* Do you like it? *(Applause.)* Thank you. Thank you. *(Vera sits and lights a cigarette. Brad has the slick, yet breezy conversational style of the period.)*

BRAD. Your dress, is how should I put it … very colorful.

VERA. Colorful? Is that the best you can do, darling? How long have you been hosting this show? Colorful is how you describe a trip to Tijuana. No, this is an original by Alexander Wynn. *(To audience.)* Isn't it wonderful? He's a fabulous young Negro designer.

BRAD. Really? A young Negro designer, you say?

VERA. Yes, he is a Negro, I know I am supposed to say, what is it? Um, um Afro-American. But, forgive me, I find it to be a very cumbersome word. A mouthful, honey. I'll probably get a letter from the NAACP tomorrow morning. But try as I might, this old tongue just can't be retrained. And, let me tell you something, I marched with Dr. King, of course I did. And I was one of the very first actresses in Hollywood to be outspoken about the civil rights movement in the '50s. If you remember, I publicly turned down the role of Hanna Gunn in the film *The Ghost of Alabama.*

BRAD. I remember the controversy.

VERA. But, I didn't come here to talk about that, right now I'm hopelessly in love with this Negro designer, Alexander Wynn —

BRAD. Spectacular —

VERA. And I told him I would wear his dress on your show.

PETER. Your dress is really groovy, I almost wore something like it to the show.

BRAD. Isn't that funny, so did I. *(Studio audience laughter.)*

VERA. And who is this dashing young man? *(Studio applause and a few screams.)* Are you an actor? *(Peter laughs, she should know who he is, but she clearly doesn't.)*

PETER. No, I play rock and roll. The blues. *(Audience screams.)*

VERA. Rock and roll?! The blues? Really?

BRAD. So, now you're conducting this interview, are you? *(Studio audience laughter.)*

VERA. I'm just asking this handsome young man some questions, because we were never formally introduced by the wretched host of this television show. *(Vera takes hold of Peter's arm as she speaks.)*

BRAD. *(To audience.)* That would be me. *(Audience laughter.)*

VERA. Call me old-fashioned, but I like to know who I'm addressing.

BRAD. Vera Stark, meet Peter Rhys-Davies. Peter Rhys-Davies meet Vera Stark.

PETER. I'm a huge fan of the *The Belle of New Orleans*. I saw it on the tellie in me hotel room, like, last summer. I really loved it, dug it. It was really, really moving, you know it surprised me. I cried at the end, I'm not ashamed. When you said to her, what is um, um … "Stay awake" … um, um —

BRAD. Oh, Vera, you know I won't let you leave until we hear the line. *(Applause.)* Oh please.

VERA. *(Flirtatiously.)* It's only because I'm fond of you. *(Dramatically.)* "Stay awake, and together we'll face a new day." *(Thunderous studio audience applause.)*

BRAD. That line just gets me every time.

VERA. Oh shut up. I've made over fifty-five pictures since that time. Some good ones. *The Confederates* with the late great Arthur Potter, *God's Fitful Chilluns* with Jerome McGregor and my dear friend Lottie McBride, and of course I did the series *Lumus and Larry.* But all that anyone seems to remember is *The Belle of New Orleans. (Audience applause.)*

BRAD. Well, it is the picture that first introduced you to an audience, and you were nominated for a rather big shiny award. And I have to say, that time has not diminished the magic of that film. I caught it on television not so long ago, and I found myself watching the whole darn thing, even though I've seen it a half-dozen times. I mean, everyone's little Sweetie Pie, Gloria Mitchell, just magical, and the Brazilian spitfire actress Anna Maria Fernandez … Your cast was just … just phenomenal. *(Vera smiles knowingly, and reaches for a pitcher of water on the end table.)*

VERA. Can I drink this? Is this here for me?

BRAD. Are you trying to change the subject, Vera?

VERA. It's been the subject of my life for the last forty years, of course I'm trying to change the subject. *(Vera begins to pour herself a glass of water.)*

HERB. *(Regarding* The Brad Donovan Show.*)* Pause. Carmen, Afua … quick, what happened to Vera Stark?

AFUA. She got tired. She got angry. She got, how should I say it? She got real. She got real. She got radicalized.

CARMEN. I love that my colleague is a romantic. No, Vera didn't move to Cuba and cut sugar cane, she was simply pulled in many directions, forced to contend with the inherent contradiction that was —

HERB. Hold onto that thought, I want to come back to this, but let's push into the interview. *(Studio. 1973.)*

BRAD. Vera, I know our audience is just dying to know what you've been up to. *(She gives him a "get real" look.)*

VERA. Well, after years of neglect, someone saw fit to pull me out of a dusty old trunk.

BRAD. Oh, that's not true.

VERA. Oh shut up, it's true. It's so true it hurts. But after years of wandering the desert, so to speak, out of the blue Howard Martin called and invited me to be part of the Folies Bergere in Vegas. It's a marvelous show. And I simply jumped at the opportunity to perform again. And I hadn't realized how much I really, really missed it. And it feels wonderful to be back working the strip.

PETER. Vegas is one wild weird place. The lights, crazy. Craziness.

VERA. Woo! Yes! And you know, I haven't performed live since I toured Germany with the Petie Owens Orchestra. *(Vera lights another cigarette and laughs, very self-amused.)*

BRAD. I believe there's an album from that tour.

VERA. Yes, we recorded a wonderful live album.

PETER. I love that. You know, live, you get the audience and stuff. You know, like, ya. *(Peter leaps to his feet. Belts —)*

PETER. *(Sings.)*
    There is something I love about that gal of mine,
    There is something I love about that gal of mine,
(The unseen band joins in with a bluesy riff.)
    There is something I love about that gal of mine,
    She treats me right and loves me all of the time.
Yeah. *(Audience screams.)*

BRAD. Amazing. Yes. The element of surprise. *(Peter laughs and sits down.)*

VERA. Honey, I want one of his happy pills. *(Vera laughs.)*

BRAD. You and me both. So Vera, are you working on a new picture?

VERA. I'm going to tell you something … there's nothing worthwhile being made today. The pictures aren't true quality like the old days. Now, well, it's all crap with guns, bad language and bikinis …

PETER. I'd love to see you in a bikini. *(Audience laughter.)*

VERA. Honey, I don't think you can handle all of this. Have you ever been with a Negro woman or man? Because these days, you know —

BRAD. Oh Vera.

VERA. What? Can I say these things on television? Young man I kissed one white man in my life. Look at that, the audience has gotten silent. I hope they don't cancel you, but I'm going to finish my story —

BRAD. Vera, why don't you tell us about —

VERA. Oh hush up, I kissed this actor, I won't say his name, you can read it in my autobiography. But we shared a tender gin fueled kiss at the Club Alhambra.

BRAD. Yes, fascinating, um, but —

VERA. It was the spontaneous response to a rather memorable evening. The Buzz Mulligan Orchestra was swinging and we just completely forgot ourselves. It practically caused a riot. True story. It was a harmless kiss. This was before those pippies —

BRAD. You mean hippies —

VERA. Yes, hippies introduced the notion of free love. No, back then love came with a price. *(Peter Rhys-Davies laughs.)*

PETER. I like you.

VERA. I like you.

PETER. You tell it like it is.

VERA. Yes, I do.

BRAD. Speaking of love, you were married to two rather famous gentlemen, weren't you —

VERA. Are you reading those questions from a card? Must we bring up unfortunate things? Yes. Leroy, my first husband, was a brilliant musician. But, he … he got himself into a little trouble, as you might remember.

BRAD. Yes. Yes.

VERA. He was backed into a corner, and he came out fighting. Young people don't know this, but we had to be fighters back then. Celestial Pictures terminated my contract because of my relationship with Leroy. Betcha didn't know that, honey.

BRAD. No, no, I didn't.

VERA. But, I make no apologies for him, and I understand why what happened happened. You're looking at me, but I had that kind of unfortunate love for Leroy, and it's only after a couple cocktails and a sedative that I make peace with it.

BRAD. Are you saying that what he did was right?

VERA. I was there, and in that moment he was like a lovely April shower that suddenly and unexpectedly turns into a squall and blows everything away. He reacted humanly, too humanly perhaps. I don't know. Leroy was a major talent, so were many of us. But … but … Yes, I'm sorry for the man who was on the dark side of his historic rage, but it happened. *(The lights abruptly shift. The colloquium. Three academics sit on the stage, Carmen, Herb and Afua.)*

HERB. Hmmm. What happened to Vera Stark?

AFUA. *(Suddenly.)* Dark … side … of his historic rage. Dark side of his historic rage! *(Without a breath.)* Darksideofhishistoricraaaaggggee! Look at the expression on Brad Donovan's face. Isn't it deliciousssss? He doesn't know what to say. She's challenging them to understand Leroy's historic rage. Remember, these sort of things don't get said on popular television. 1973. There's no apprehension in her voice. She's fearless. Fearless! It's 1973, Cliff Lloyd took four white racist cops hostage. The country was on fire, and this woman is talking about kissing a white man —

CARMEN. Who we now know from her autobiography was none other than Dudley Dumar.

AFUA. She's a volcano on the verge of erupting, ready to release the pressure of years of battling patriarchal hegemony. And she begins by provoking the younger generation, by asking Peter Rhys-Davies whether, indeed, he's ready for a more progressive relationship to race and sexual orientation. She is a rebel! A warrior! She is saying whitey, WHITEY! Pay attention to this "nigger" woman.

HERB. Interesting, unpack it for me.

AFUA. What happened to Vera Stark? *(Recited.)*
    Representations of self,
    truth unfurled like strips of mud cloth,
    laid across a bare black back of a Nubian goddess,
    She, chanting, I am here … bitches —

CARMEN. Poetics aside. I'd like to steer the conversation back to the question.

AFUA. Should I get out of your way?

CARMEN. I don't want to step on you. Indeed, if I'm reading this interview correctly, I recognize the immensity of Vera's struggle. A little context for the audience. I'm a semiotician and a classically trained actress, I studied acting with Tomas Gorog in Stuttgart. And as you can see, I'm a woman of a certain girth, so I know how easy it is to be ascribed a role and become imprisoned by it. At the Academy I played Juliet, Nora, Medea, classical roles, but in the professional world I'm offered the same crumbs that in many respects defined Vera's career.

AFUA. And your point is?

CARMEN. *"Das unausgesprochene,"* to cite Arnhelm Machenhauer, "The unspoken!"

HERB. Interesting.

CARMEN. The coded silence.

HERB. Mmm.

CARMEN. If we watch the interview carefully. It's not just what's said, but also the tension of what's unspoken.

HERB. Mm. What are you getting at?

CARMEN. The internal tug of war, between what she was and could have been, and what she has come to represent. What am I getting at? What am I getting at? *(Growing excited and passionate.)* Vera had a very difficult career. Many ups and downs. She battled alcoholism. Bankruptcy.

HERB. I believe we have some images from the period. Would you please? *(A quick montage of photos play as Carmen speaks: A publicity shot from* Lumus and Larry. *A publicity of Vera from the zombie movie, a still of Lottie and Vera from God's Fitful Chilluns. A publicity shot of Leroy Barksdale and Vera dancing intimately. Drunk Vera in a cocktail dress slumped on a curb. A mugshot of Leroy.)*

CARMEN. Thank you. She had two problematic marriages. One to Dortch Ross, a middleweight prize fighter and world-class philanderer. And of course there was her marriage to Leroy Barksdale the trumpeter for the Petie Owens Orchestra. As we all know, he ended up doing a stint in prison for manslaughter.

HERB. Yes. He accidentally beat a drunk heckler to death with his trumpet.

CARMEN. Barksdale was a rabble-rouser, an early and outspoken critic of racism in Hollywood. Vera's career took a major hit, because she stood by him throughout his troubles.

HERB. Hmm. I don't entirely agree with that, and I'm gonna say something that's gonna make you angry, Carmen. You can't *(Sing-*

song.) blame, blame, blame Barksdale for the decline of Vera's career, she squandered the goodwill of audiences both black and white, by taking demeaning roles // in second-rate films.

CARMEN. Her options were finite!

AFUA. Yo, but she infused // those films —

CARMEN. Do we have the Barksdale footage?! *(Weathered documentary footage of Leroy, older, worn. He smokes a cigarette. His voice is raspy from years of booze, a heroin addiction and neglect.)*

FRENCH DOCUMENTARY MAKER. *(Offscreen.)* Mr. Barksdale, it is a honor to finally meet you.

LEROY. You ain't the first cat to come in here asking questions. Where you from, Paris? I been to Paris, if you know what I'm saying. Par-ee. *(Leroy laughs, inside joke.)*

FRENCH DOCUMENTARY MAKER. *(Offscreen.)* Tell me about that night on August third.

LEROY. A lot of folks ask about that night. I don't want to talk about it! I said I don't want to talk about it! Okay, if you ask me again, I'll walk the hell outta here. We clear?! *(Leroy starts to get up.)*

FRENCH DOCUMENTARY MAKER. *(Offscreen.)* Then, talk to me about Vera Stark.

LEROY. Vera. Vera Stark. Mmmm. She was beautiful. And a damn good actress. A lot of folks don't know that. Wanna hear a little story about Vera? She was making a film with that, um, that um, German actress, you know with the deep voice. And of course, Vera was playing a maid. The costume designer had dressed her up in this ridiculous maid's uniform, made her look like a pickanniny for Ole Virginny. But, Vera had the costume mistress take in the dress two inches around the waist and the hips, so it looked real sexy. And I could tell the director dug it, 'cuz when you see the film, there are all these wonderful close-ups of Vera bending over to pick up laundry. She knew how to work all angles, get a little more than they was willing to give her. *(Leroy demonstrates for the camera.)* I used to tease Vera, you know, joke that she was cheesecake served in a brown paper bag. She was something else back then. Beautiful. Smart. Knew it. Let me tell you something real, I loved that woman, but Hollywood, it didn't treat her right. You want the truth? Ask Vera about Gloria Mitchell, if you really want to know about the Hollywood game? Can you get that damn light out of my eyes.

CARMEN. *"Das unausgesprochene."* Can we continue with the interview, please. *(Lights shift.)*

Scene 3

Television studio, 1973. Vera, Brad and Peter. Studio audience applause.

BRAD. Welcome back, I'm sitting here with Peter Rhys-Davies and Vera Stark. And I have someone else who is very eager to join us. Vera, an old friend of yours found out that you were on the show and insisted on joining us.

VERA. Really, I didn't know I had any friends left? *(Audience laughter.)*

BRAD. Please give a warm round of applause to "America's Original Sweetie Pie" ... Gloria Mitchell. *(Gloria, sixties, wearing a red dress, a fabulous fur coat, dressed to kill and smoking a cigarette. She has a tinge of a British accent from years of living abroad. Vera is genuinely shocked. She stands and covers her mouth.)*

VERA. My goodness. My, my, Gloria!

GLORIA. *(Dramatically.)* Vera! *(The two women embrace.)*

VERA. This is a surprise. I am shocked. I am flabbergasted.

GLORIA. How long has it been?

VERA. A long time, honey. Look at you. You look marvelous, but you always did know how to wear a fur. *(Gloria shows off her fur coat.)*

GLORIA. And you look absolutely gorgeous. You wicked woman, you haven't aged a second. *(Brad ushers the two women over to the seating area.)*

PETER. *(Suddenly.)* You're Gloria Mitchell?! *The Belle of New Orleans!*

GLORIA. Yes!

PETER. Whoa, I thought you was dead.

GLORIA. That's the problem with this town, you don't die once, you're forced to die many slow deaths.

VERA. Well, you look wonderful for a corpse.

GLORIA. It's all an illusion, I'm held together with powder and paste, scratch a little deeper and I'll crumble.

VERA. Won't we all, honey. Won't we all. *(Gloria gives Vera her handbag to hold as she takes off her coat. A moment. The women sit.)*

GLORIA. I flew in from London only yesterday, but I had to see you, darling.

BRAD. And we are thrilled.

GLORIA. Thank you.

VERA. I haven't seen you since we did *Five Stolen Kisses.*

GLORIA. No, no. That can't be possible. That was the last film I appeared in before I moved to London.

BRAD. Golly, is that true? It was a delightful film. So, Gloria, tell me, how long have you lived in London?

GLORIA. Twenty years. I moved there with my third husband, Malcolm Braithwaite, who is of course the conductor of the London Symphony Orchestra. Quite a difference from Hollywood, and I love it. *(Gloria waves to the audience. Vera rolls her eyes.)*

BRAD. You know, people talk about the wonderfully warm rapport that you two had in *The Belle of New Orleans.* And I was wondering, how long have you known each other?

GLORIA. Don't tell him. Don't you dare tell!

BRAD. I'm sure I'm not the only one who wants to know. Audience? *(Applause. Audience laughter.)*

GLORIA. Vera is one of the few people who knew me before I even understood the meaning of the word glamour.

VERA. Don't believe her, this woman came out the womb wearing pearls and a fur coat. *(Gloria, laughs, basking in the audience applause.)*

BRAD. I want to put something to rest, is there any truth to the rumor that you worked as Gloria's maid?

VERA. Yes, believe it or not, I was her maid.

GLORIA. And dear friend.

VERA. And maid. Gloria caught a break, and I had to catch the bus to work every day, honey. It was the Depression, this one here is too young to remember, but people were standing in bread lines. You took work where you could find it. And we ... were troopers, we did what we had to do. *(Gloria laughs uncomfortably.)*

GLORIA. Yes darling, but, you make it sound horrible, it was a gorgeous time.

VERA. In many ways, yes, but it wasn't easy for everyone, honey. And tell 'em the truth, we go a little further back than that. *(A moment.)*

GLORIA. Yes, well, the audience is going to chuckle, but we were youngsters on the vaudeville circuit.

BRAD. You're kidding.

GLORIA. You remember those days, Vera. A caravan of acts, one more ridiculous than the next. *(Gloria launches into an old African American vaudeville song like "I'm Just Wild About Harry.")*

    I'm just wild about Harry
    And Harry's wild about me!
    The heav'nly blisses of his kisses,
    Fills me with ecstasy!

C'mon Vera, you remember. *(Vera is prompted to take a verse, then the women joyfully sing together. Brad signals for the unseen band to accompany them.)*

VERA. *(Sings.)*

    He's sweet just like chocolate candy,
    Or like the honey from the bee
    Oh, I'm just wild about Harry,
    And he's just wild about me.

(The unseen band comes in.)

VERA and GLORIA. *(Singing.)*

    Now I'm just wild about Harry
    And Harry's wild about me!
    The heav'nly blisses of his kisses,
    Fills me with ecstasy!

(They battle for the spotlight.)

    Say now he's sweet just like chocolate candy,
    Or like the honey from a bee
    Oh, I'm just wild about Harry,
    And he's just wild about, cannot do without,
    He's just wild about me.

(Applause. The women hug.)

BRAD. Gloria Mitchell, Vera Stark! Wonderful! Many of our great performers got their feet wet on the vaudeville stage. Bunny Briggons, the Carlson Brothers. It's fascinating, I didn't realize the circuit was integrated back when you two were performing as children. *(A moment. Vera glances to Gloria for a response.)*

GLORIA. Who can remember?! That was ancient history. We were performers first and foremost. Show people.

VERA. Yes, but there was something called the TOBA circuit, don't remember what it stands for, but we used to joke it meant Tough on Black Asses.

GLORIA. Oh, Vera, it was so long ago, these young people have no idea what you're talking about. *(Gloria is clearly growing uncomfortable.)*

VERA. Toby time, you know, // Negro vaudeville where —

BRAD. Gloria, what brings you back to Los Angeles?

GLORIA. Oh nothing, I'm just being honored with the United Motion Picture's Medal of Honor.

BRAD. That's fantastic! *(Applause. Gloria acknowledges the audience.)*

GLORIA. *(Whispers.)* Thank you.

VERA. Congratulations, forty years in this business, you get a medal of honor, and I get a two-week engagement in Vegas. Miss Gloria Mitchell, folks.

GLORIA. You joke, but I welcome every opportunity I get to come back here, because this town has been so very good to me. Even though I couldn't get work here for many years. They'll give you awards, but they won't give you a job. *(She takes Vera's hand.)* And of course, I wanted to see this marvelously talented woman. I've invited her to visit London a half-dozen times, but she never comes.

VERA. Honey, my phone hasn't rang since 1969 when I was asked to do some dreadful zombie picture in Haiti.

GLORIA. Oh, the same old Vera. I do love you, I hope you know that.

BRAD. I want to share something, I have a slide of the two of you in *The Belle of New Orleans. (A projected slide of Vera and Gloria in* The Belle of New Orleans.*)*

GLORIA. Look at us. That is just so incredible. We look like babies. Oh god, I remember that costume, they had me in the tightest corset I didn't think I'd be able to make it through the scene. It was an impossible scene, and I was terribly nervous, and I'd eaten an enormous lunch that day.

VERA. She won't tell you this, but Gloria gained fifteen pounds while we were filming this picture, so when you see me struggling with her corset, honey, I was really struggling. *(Audience laughter.)*

BRAD. When you look at these old pictures, what's running through your mind?

VERA. Too many things. It was such an interesting, difficult and wonderful time. // I was trying —

GLORIA. Every actress at the studio wanted to be in this picture, you know. It's a remarkable film, and it's a tribute to the director Maxmillian Von Oster, who fought for his vision. I adore him for it —

VERA. And not many people know this, but I fought tooth and nail for the last line in *The Belle of New Orleans.*

BRAD. Really? I can't believe that.

PETER. Crazy. Artists, like, they don't trust that we have a complete vision, right?

VERA. They didn't want Tilly, a Negro woman, to have the final word. The studio tried to cut the line.

BRAD. Thank God they didn't.

VERA. They felt the words were too um … um … ambiguous. It may not seem so today, but the film was very daring for its time. It was banned in most theatres in the South.

BRAD. But correct me if I'm wrong, the film also came under some criticism from the NAACP, particularly for the depiction of the role of Tilly. *(A moment.)*

GLORIA. Unfairly, I think. Vera was incredible in that role. She raised the bar for all of us.

VERA. *(Agitated.)* And people forget that I opened doors in Hollywood. Yes, I did! I marched with Dr. King in Selma. I wore a dashiki before Malcolm X. I've had to battle all of my career! It's easy for people to point fingers today, but honey, should I not have taken that role and cleaned toilets and made beds in someone's home instead?!

HERB. If you please. Dashiki before Malcolm X. *(Vera and company freeze. Colloquium.)* This was Vera's final interview. As we know, her show at the Folies Bergère, billed as her triumphant comeback, was cut short because of her repeated absences due to her alcoholism. She infamously did a striptease onstage and was arrested for public indecency.

AFUA. Booze wasn't the source of the problem, Brother Herb. She was shackled to the stage, and paraded like chattel. Bottom line, she couldn't, wouldn't do it anymore.

CARMEN. *(Shouts.)* She was doing what she loved, but she was —

HERB. Let me interrupt, I have a colleague who many years ago was visiting friends in Palm Springs, and he, um, he believes that the elderly maid who served him dinner was none other than Vera Stark.

CARMEN. There have been Vera sightings for years, she's a maid, she's a crossing guard in Tuscaloosa. *(Afua rises abruptly.)*

AFUA. Please, apocrypha! The fact is that on November 17th, 1973, Vera took a deadly cocktail of booze and pills. A defiant "fuck you" to the industry. She died in a hotel room in Reno. She went to her grave misidentified as a prostitute named Shirley "Treasure" Bowers.

CARMEN. Show me the evidence.

AFUA. Read my book, I write extensively about it in my collection of essays, *Interrogating Mammy, the Parenthetical Negro Dilemma.*

HERB. Bottom line, did Vera take her own life in a seedy Reno hotel? Carmen, your thoughts?

CARMEN. Well, several years ago, I got a call from a college friend who worked in a homeless shelter in Santa Monica. She said, "You're not going to believe this, but there's an old woman who's been coming in for about a week, and she claims to be Vera Stark." I thought she was pulling my leg, but you see, I'd just begun doing research for my thesis on African-American actresses in early Hollywood, so I drove down to the shelter. And there sitting in the recreation room was a small, fragile old lady with these beautifully expressive eyes, and I knew immediately it was her. *(A moment. Carmen's eyes fill with tears.)* I'm sorry, I get a little choked up.

HERB. Take your time. Take your time.

CARMEN. It was truly heartbreaking, to see this giant talent, our own Hollywood legend, reduced to handouts. I introduced myself, told her what I was working on and her eyes just lit up. It was as if I'd offered her twenty more years of life. Please, cue the photo that I clipped from the *Santa Monica Digest. (A poor quality slide of an old bag lady who may or may not be Vera.)*

HERB. Mmmm. I'm looking at the photo, and frankly speaking it could be … anyone.

CARMEN. Exactly. But it isn't. Enlarge please. *(Photo is enlarged, close up on the eyes, a grainy, degenerated image.)*

AFUA. That's a bag lady in Santa Monica, she —

CARMEN. It's Vera. It's her. I talked to her for hours. About her husbands, her friends, the studio system … She talked about everything, in no particular order, and with no sense of chronology or priority. Random anecdotes. In truth, it was the ramblings of an old woman desperate to be remembered. But, she talked mostly about her cousin, sometimes with disgust, sometimes with awe. A girl who she performed with in the early days on the vaudeville circuit, when the Stark family had a popular song and dance team. Vera seemed to suggest that her cousin had the career that she herself deserved. I wrote a little about this conversation in my recent book *Hollywood Dreams.*

HERB. It's a wonderful book by the way, and in it you claim that Vera's cousin was none other than the screen legend … Gloria

Mitchell. *(Afua shakes her head.)*

AFUA. Well, I've struggled through your book, and with all due respect, my sister, I think you've done some brilliant creative writing. There's no written or anecdotal evidence to support this claim.

CARMEN. That isn't —

AFUA. In fact, we know that Vera worked as Gloria's maid, and as to the nature of their relationship, I think it's safe to say that it was probably that of mistress and servant. Missy and mammy.

HERB. Interesting. In Dr. Eugene Clarkson's book *Sexual Misadventures in Black Hollywood*, it's suggested that Gloria and Vera were lesbian lovers. That it was a torrid affair, that ended badly after Vera was nominated for an Academy Award. Some point to the unique and fiery chemistry of the two actresses in *The Belle of New Orleans*, as the reason why the film succeeds.

CARMEN. No, Herb, I've made a very strong case for them being cousins.

HERB. Kissing cousins.

CARMEN. Cousins. The interview is very telling. Cousins. And I think we miss something key, if we don't examine their careers in that context. // If —

AFUA. Of course, of course it's the thesis of your book, so I know how strongly you feel about this, but I disagree. As a black lesbian, I want nothing more than to claim Vera. But, yo, can Vera not exist without a relationship to Gloria? C'mon y'all, why do my colleagues insist on framing the conversation in these reductionist terms. I'm not gonna allow Gloria to hijack our discussion about Vera. It's too easy. White women hijacked Vera's career. Fuck Gloria Mitchell!

HERB. Hold onto that thought. Let's roll footage. *(Studio, 1973.)*

BRAD. I didn't mean to stir the pot. Over the years you've brought us many delightful characters, and I for one am a huge fan of *The Belle of New Orleans*, and I can't imagine it any other way.

VERA. Thank you.

BRAD. We ... We don't have much time left, and I know this has been an emotional reunion —

VERA. I'm still in shock. You can't do these sort of things to a woman my age.

BRAD. I wanted to ask you one final question. You've both had really interesting and varied careers. Gloria, you were one of the biggest and brightest stars in Hollywood, and Vera, well, you ... you

lit up scenes with your memorable sassy presence. I wanted to —
GLORIA. Before you finish, can I share a terrible secret with the audience?
VERA. … Gloria?
GLORIA. No, let me finish —
VERA. What are —
GLORIA. I … I wasn't going to share this, but the moment seems right. *(Vera smiles, surprised, suddenly nervous.)*
VERA. Honey, here, now? If you —
GLORIA. No, let me. I've been hesitant to say this for a long time. And I think I owe my fans and everyone here the truth, I … I am … formally retiring from acting. Yes. *(The audience gasps. Vera is shocked, it isn't the confession she was expecting.)* And I wanted to say, here, live on television, that I owe a great deal to this marvelous woman. Vera, I know I should have told you that years ago.
VERA. Oh, stop the theatrics, you're not auditioning for anything.
GLORIA. I beg your pardon?!
VERA. "Boating on the bayou!" Retiring, you couldn't give up acting if your life depended on it. And you know exactly what I'm talking about!
PETER. I have no idea what you two are talking about.
GLORIA. I mean it, Vera, I've always envied her talent and drive.
VERA. My talent? What has all of my enviable talent given me? Mammy Jane, Josie, Bitsy, Petunia and Addie, forty years of characters who they didn't even bother to give last names. That's something to celebrate, honey!
GLORIA. Oh, don't be droll.
VERA. You know you've had a wonderfully perfect career, so I'd rather you didn't talk to me about envy. Not now, not ever!
BRAD. Gloria, I read somewhere that —
GLORIA. I'm here, because I —
VERA. It's me you're talking to, honey.
GLORIA. *(Exasperated, old Gloria creeps in.)* Oh, Vera, Vera, Vera.
VERA. Oh calm yourself, you spoiled pampered rotten potato. And I've wanted to say that for a long time.
GLORIA. A rotten potato? What the hell does that mean?
VERA. Oh, you know what it means, Gloria. *(Gloria stands.)*
GLORIA. Really?! *(Vera stands.)*
VERA. Really!
BRAD. Gloria, Vera, when you two were —

58

VERA. *(Shouts.)* You have no idea what it was like for me!

GLORIA. *(Shouts.)* You have no idea what it was like for me! *(The women rise with their emotions.)*

VERA. I do. Don't forget, I was there. But, you … you could have —

GLORIA. Don't you dare say it!

BRAD. I was —

VERA. "America's Little Sweetie Pie," I cleaned up after you, didn't I? Just quietly watched you do what you had to do. And I know what you did, // honey.

GLORIA. You! // You! —

VERA. But, I didn't say anything, waiting, hoping that you'd —

GLORIA. You better be careful —

VERA. Your success mean the world to me, but never once did you turn back around to consider the rest of us —

GLORIA. You are out of line, stop it! If you say one more word, you hypocrite, I swear I will —

VERA. What?!

BRAD. Ladies, ladies, why don't we sit down.

PETER. I don't know what you two old birds are fighting about, but this is trippy.

BRAD. Have a seat. Ladies, I was about to throw in the towel. *(Audience laughter.)* When you were making *The Belle of New Orleans,* did you have any idea of the impact that it would have on audiences?

GLORIA. *(Recovering.)* It was a great script. I knew it the first time I read it. I couldn't put it down.

BRAD. And you, Vera?

VERA. *(Still emotional.)* How could we know? How could we? But, it's funny, I played the role of Tilly, a slave woman bound to her mistress, and here, all of these years later, and I find myself bound to Tilly, a slave woman. I wish I could shake that silly little wench out of me. But here we are nearly forty years later, still … still answering questions about that picture. I've lived a lifetime since I made it. But, Tilly … Tilly is my shame and … my glory. She birthed me into a career. Perhaps I had to play her to get where I am. I don't know. *(Whispered.)* I don't know.

GLORIA. Oh darling, if people only knew what it was like at the beginning.

VERA. They wouldn't believe you, if you told them.

GLORIA. Forgive me, Vera?

VERA. For what, honey?

GLORIA. Oh, for not being better in touch. For taking you for granted all of these years. I wish things had … well … I missed you, terribly.

VERA. Yes, well … life. *(Gloria takes Vera's hand.)*

BRAD. And on that poignant note, it's that time again. I'd like to thank my guests, Peter Rhys-Davies, Vera Stark // and — *(Vera and company freeze. Show jingle. Light shifts. Colloquium.)*

HERB. And the footage ends there. Thoughts?

AFUA. Bottom line. Vera made a film that still draws huge ratings when it's broadcast on television. A film that occasionally makes me cringe when I see it, but I will confess that every time Vera appears on the screen I get giddy, I get excited. Why?

HERB. Clearly, // because she —

AFUA. Because, when I watch Vera act, I'm watching a young woman, an artist, grappling with representations of self. Who am I? Who am I? —

CARMEN. Yes and no. // Yes and no.

HERB. Vera may have been a promising actress, but over the years she has presented such a contradictory narrative of self. It's hard to say who she really was. // Because,

CARMEN. Yes, but Vera believed that she was breathing fresh life into painful stereotypes, but ultimately she was … was denied agency.

HERB. Even so, the Vera I know was aiding and abetting Hollywood's // distortion of history.

AFUA. Yo, my girl battled writers, // directors and producers who had no clue and little interest in who she was.

CARMEN.	HERB.
So can we solely hold her responsible for perpetuating images // that have come to define how people still view African American women on the screen today?	We all agree Vera was simply breathtaking in *The Belle of New Orleans,* but ultimately she still she was just another shucking, jiving, // fumbling, mumbling, laughing, shuffling, pancake-making mammy in the kitchen.

AFUA. Stop! NO! My girl may have been many things, but she refused to be reduced // to an image on the screen.

HERB. Theories! Rumors! Conjecture! I don't give a goddamn! The images remain problematic. And those images are indelible, and they can't simply be apologized away —

CARMEN. *(Passionately.)* But we have to actively engage with them, listen to them and understand why they exist, and perhaps what the performer was attempting to tell us about the ethos of the time — *(We hear the gentle audio of* The Belle of New Orleans *beneath the colloquium.)*

VERA. Mis Marie. Mis Marie! // Talk to me. Mis Marie. Oh Lawdy mis please don't die on me, you can't leave me, what will Tilly do without her mis'? Ya remember when we wuz younguns running barefoot in the back yard and you dun found dat wounded bird, and Mammy said let it die, but ya … ya taught dat poor thang to fly again. Well, you dat bird, and I ain't gonna let you go without a fight. Fight! *(Carmen rises to meet Afua's energy.)*

AFUA. She was interrogating the medium from the inside —

CARMEN. Yes, but remember she was also fragile, human, an actress playing a role. Are we demanding too much of her?!

HERB. What happened to Vera Stark? In the words of that wise old sage Grandford Ellis, "History is a question constantly being rephrased." *(Light shift. The movie. Black and white.* The Belle of New Orleans. *A richly appointed Southern boudoir, circa 1855. Gloria, playing the role of sickly Marie, the octoroon mistress of a wealthy merchant, sits up in bed.)*

GLORIA. I have no more fight, Tilly.

MAX. *(Offstage.)* No. no. no! Cut.

VERA. I ain't gonna let you go. Don't die mis', don't die. You the only thing I's got. Mis' Marie.

MAX. *(Offstage.)* Cut. What is happening? This is no good. Ladies, please step out for camera adjustment! *(The women step out of screen onto stage, Young Vera and Gloria from* The Belle of New Orleans. *Activity whirls around them, cameras shift.)*

MAX. *(Offstage.)* Ladies.

VERA. *(Exasperated.)* C'mon let's run lines. *(Gloria smiles.)*

GLORIA. Hey Vera, you remember that place in Brooklyn?

VERA. Which one?

GLORIA. The run-down joint where the guy who owned it was always drunk and wanted you to play his organ. *(Vera fights the urge to smile.)*

VERA. Yeah, I remember. Did you ever play it?

GLORIA. Vera, shame, you know I didn't learn to play the organ until I was much older. *(Vera laughs.)*

VERA. What made you think of that?

GLORIA. I was just thinking what if ... that's all, what if ... you know, what if we'd stayed back in Brooklyn with Granny and the whole crew. You know. It's funny how things work out.

VERA. Ain't it. Honey, can I ask you something?

GLORIA. Sure, sugar, what is it?

VERA. You know at the end of the scene.

GLORIA. Yes?

VERA. You know where you say, "I'm free, Tilly." Well, I'm having trouble, I can't find that last line, and I was thinking, and I know Maxmillian has told us a million times that the moment is about being freed from life and its burdens, but ... but it seems —

GLORIA. What?

VERA. Well, what if in that moment Marie is sharing with Tilly what it means to be free of slavery. You know, Free.

GLORIA. Yes, I see, but isn't that moment about Marie?

VERA. Yes, Marie is finally liberated, and she's telling Tilly for the first time what it means to be free of prejudice. Truly free.

GLORIA. But, for God's sake, how will anybody know that?

VERA. We will. *(A moment.)*

GLORIA. *(Emotional.)* Yes. I ... like that. *(Gloria thinks. Contemplates.)* "I'm free, Tilly. I'm free!" Yes! *(Gloria makes an adjustment.)* "I'm free, Tilly. I'm free."

VERA. "Stay awake ... and together we'll face a new day."

MAX. *(Offstage.)* Ladies. Are ready? *(The women step back into* The Belle of New Orleans. *SLATE:* "The Belle of New Orleans. *Take Five." The camera moves in on Vera, thinking, preparing, questioning.)*

MAX. *(Offstage.)* Sound. Camera. Action. *(Camera moves into Vera's face on the verge. Colloquium.)*

End of Play

PROPERTY LIST

Glass of gin
Script
Dish of chocolates
Cigarettes, lighter
Green gown
Labels, men's shirts, needle and thread
6 cigarettes, lighter
Purse with script
Cigarettes, lighters
Vase with azaleas
Bottles of liquor
Gin bottle
Martini glasses
Bucket of ice and sliced lemons
Pillows
Empty plate
Seltzer with lime
Lemonade
Tray of glasses
Broom
Pitcher of water, glasses
Handbag

SOUND EFFECTS

Radio program
Songs from the 1930s
Doorbell
1970s television show music
Studio audience applause and laughter
Bluesy riff